GEORGETOWN PEABODY LIBRARY

3 2120 00034 732 6

W9-AAV-879

AVIATION:
REACHING
FOR THE
SKY

AVIATION: REACHING FOR THE SKY

Don Berliner

The Oliver Press, Inc.
Minneapolis

Copyright © 1997 by The Oliver Press, Inc.

All rights reserved.
No part of this book may be reproduced in any form or by
any means without permission in writing from the publisher.
Please address inquiries to:

The Oliver Press, Inc.
Charlotte Square
5707 West 36th Street
Minneapolis, MN 55416-2510

Library of Congress Cataloging-in-Publication Data
Berliner, Don
Aviation: reaching for the sky / Don Berliner
p. cm. — (Innovators)
    Contents: The Montgolfier brothers and the hot air balloon—
Henri Giffard and the dirigible—Otto Lilienthal and the
ornithopter—Samuel Pierpont Langley and the aerodrome— The
Wright brothers and the airplane—Glenn Curtiss and the seaplane—
Igor Sikorsky and the helicopter.
Includes bibliographical references and index.
ISBN 1-881508-33-1 (lib. bdg.)
1. Aeronautics—Biography—Juvenile literature. [1. Aeronautics—
Biography.] I. Title. II. Series
TL539.B455 1996
629.13'0092—dc20
[B]

                                                              96-4940
                                                                  CIP
                                                                   AC

ISBN: 1-881508-33-1
Innovators III
Printed in the United States of America

03 02 01 00 99 98   8 7 6 5 4 3 2

CONTENTS

The Will to Fly

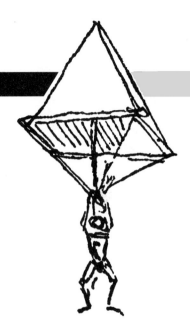

For thousands of years, people who dreamed of flying employed their powers of observation and creativity in a contest against the natural elements, the laws of physics, and the beliefs of their fellow humans. Battling the combined forces of wind, gravity, and public opinion hardly seemed like a fair fight. And, in most cases, it wasn't.

Humans who attempted to fly faced winds that were strong and unpredictable, and gravity kept their feet on the ground even when their minds were soaring in the sky. In addition, popular beliefs, which were often backed by the authority of the Church, held that if human beings were meant to fly, they would have been born with wings!

It was, however, illogical thinking and a lack of knowledge that doomed most of the early attempts to fly. Machines powered by oars or sails or flapping wings stood absolutely no chance of succeeding. One by one, these early innovations failed.

Leonardo da Vinci's fifteenth-century sketch of a parachute predated the actual demonstration of a workable parachute (in 1797) by more than 300 years.

Although he is perhaps best remembered for his famous works of art, Mona Lisa *and* The Last Supper, *Leonardo da Vinci (1452-1519) also sketched several ideas for flying machines in an attempt to figure out a way for humans to fly.*

By attaching birdlike wings and tails to their bodies, many innovators over the centuries attempted to fly like the birds they observed overhead.

ornithopter: an aircraft whose flight is powered by flapping wings, as opposed to fixed wings and propellers or jets

Yet humans continued plotting and sketching and building flying machines. After all, they reasoned, if birds and insects could fly, why couldn't humans find some way to fly as well? People who longed to fly watched these soaring creatures with envy, believing that the route to the clouds was on bird-shaped vehicles with flapping wings. Building conveyances that were similar to birds, but bigger, heavier, and more powerful than even the largest bird, seemed the obvious way to satisfy humankind's desire to fly. But this was terribly wrong.

More than 500 years ago, Leonardo da Vinci, the first great aeronautical thinker, covered hundreds of notebook pages with his brilliant ideas for flight, including parachutes, ornithopters, and even helicopters. There is no evidence that Leonardo ever built more than models of any of his creations. This is fortunate because, in spite of his genius, none of his sketches exhibits a workable system of controls for a machine once it leaves the ground. Moreover, they never suggest a source of lifting power more potent than the muscles of human arms and legs. Still, if Leonardo's notebooks had not remained hidden for hundreds of years, his knowledge of mechanics and his genius in applying science and technology to the problems of flight might have speeded up the human quest to reach the skies.

Leonardo da Vinci, however, had not been the first human to dream of flying with a mechanical device. As long ago as 400 B.C., Archytas of Tarentum (in what is now Italy) had carved a wooden bird and placed it at the end of a rotating rod.

Powered by a jet of steam, the bird whirled round and round. Although the bird never flew free, the mechanism used a crude form of jet propulsion.

As early as 1000 B.C., the Chinese were flying kites. It is said that by the twelfth century, they had constructed kites that could carry humans and be used in military operations. Around A.D. 1020,

Kites provided innovators with helpful information in designing wings for gliders and airplanes.

Eilmer, a monk at western England's Malmesbury Abbey, used a pair of hand-held wings to fly from the abbey roof. Thanks more to luck than to good engineering, he broke only his legs in his quick descent to the ground. At great personal risk, Eilmer and other "tower jumpers" of the Middle Ages (A.D. 500-1400) no doubt inspired later attempts to fly.

By the eighteenth century, creative people had come up with numerous ideas for flight, and some of them enjoyed limited success. But few would-be flyers understood the overall problem of flight or knew how to solve it. Successful travel by flying machines demanded three major aerodynamic developments: lift, thrust (power), and control. Lift

In A.D. 1260, Franciscan monk Roger Bacon suggested the possibility of filling a sphere "with ethereal air" to "float on the atmosphere as a ship on water." More than 500 years would pass before a human would take to the skies in a hot-air balloon.

In 1874, a Belgian shoemaker, Vincent de Groof, plunged to his death while attempting a free flight in his ornithopter.

On modern airplanes, **lift** is provided by sturdy wings that do not move; **thrust** (or **power**) comes from jet engines or propellers; and **control** results from movable surfaces such as rudders, ailerons, and elevators.

would make a machine rise above the earth, thrust would drive the vehicle forward, and control would keep it moving in the desired direction.

As the eighteenth century drew to a close, a few bold innovators were ready to exchange their dreaming for scientific experimentation. They first tried to uncover all of the problems involved with flying. Then they attempted to solve them, one at a time. They realized they had to master lift, thrust, and control, not by imitating a bird's structure and movements, but by creating brand-new devices that would perform the same functions mechanically.

This book chronicles the successes (and failures) of aviation innovators in their early attempts to fly. It begins with the Montgolfier brothers in France, whose hot-air balloons signaled the start of

GEORGETOWN PEABODY LIBRARY

the age of human flight in 1783, and ends with Igor Sikorsky, who realized Leonardo's centuries-old dream of taking to the sky in a helicopter.

Innovations such as hot-air balloons, airplanes, and helicopters are common today, but we need to realize that it took hundreds of years to accomplish the feat that we now take for granted: flight! After the Montgolfiers had proved that it was possible for humans to take off from and then return safely to earth, many individuals, including Henri Giffard, Otto Lilienthal, Orville and Wilbur Wright, Samuel Langley, and Glenn Curtiss, led the way to the sky.

Risking their lives, fortunes, and reputations, these brave souls persevered, and safe, fast, reliable flight became a reality as a result of their daring and innovative work. Today, we must thank each of them every time we fasten our seat belts for takeoff.

Outlandish contraptions for flight, such as this helicopter that was attached to the body, convinced many people that humans would never be able to fly.

CHAPTER ONE

The Montgolfier Brothers and the Hot-Air Balloon

Nearly everyone has seen smoke rise. Around a campfire at dusk, you can see ashes and sparks rising upwards, as if floating on the smoke produced by the fire. Walking home from school in autumn, you might see smoke rising from chimneys. This simple phenomenon could not be more apparent. But not until late in the eighteenth century would someone discover that it was possible to harness the lifting power that makes smoke rise.

Among the many who had observed smoke rising were Joseph and Étienne Montgolfier, who lived near Annonay in the south of France. They were the sons of a wealthy papermaker, and their family had been prominent paper manufacturers since the 1300s. Working together, the brothers would embark upon a project that would change the world.

Joseph and Étienne had noticed that rising smoke sometimes carried bits of unburned paper up into the air. They theorized that there might be a

Like the Wright brothers many years later, the brothers Montgolfier worked successfully as a team to build a craft that would allow humans to fly.

Thanks to their family's wealth, Joseph Michel Montgolfier, at left (1740-1810), and his younger brother Jacques Étienne (1745-1799), who was known as Étienne, had both the time and the means necessary to conduct flight experiments.

practical use for the capacity of smoke to lift more than itself. According to one story, the Montgolfier brothers once saw smoke rise from a fire, fill a woman's dress that was drying on a nearby line, and then lift the garment into the air. Seeing this made them think that smoke could lift even heavier materials along with it.

In November 1782, the brothers made their first attempt to harness the mysterious lifting power they had observed. They filled small silk bags with smoke rising from a fire and sent the bags aloft. At the time, they probably did not know that more than 70 years earlier, in 1709, Bartolomeu Laurenco de Gusmão had demonstrated a similar flying balloon in the palace of the king and queen of Portugal.

The brothers Montgolfier had no idea why their "balloons" were able to rise above the ground. They thought that perhaps they had discovered some previously unknown gas or that electricity had caused the flight. For many years, the lifting power of "smoke" was referred to as "Montgolfier's gas."

The true lifting power that had sent the Montgolfiers' balloon into the sky was not the smoke produced from the fire, as they had suspected, but the heated air. The brothers did not know that air becomes lighter as it is heated. And if this heated, or thinned, air is enclosed, as in a balloon, it attempts to "float" above the cooler air that surrounds it.

Had Joseph and Étienne Montgolfier realized that heated air was lighter than cool air and that the rising, hot air provided the lift for their balloons, they could have used an ancient discovery of Archimedes to explain the balloon's mysterious flight. Around 250 B.C., this Greek mathematician and physicist had stumbled upon the principle of buoyancy, which states that an object will float if it weighs less than the substance in which it is suspended.

Buoyancy is easily observed in water, as ships are able to float on the surface of the water, even when carrying tons of cargo. Although a fully loaded boat can be very heavy, it is still lighter than the water it displaces, and, therefore, does not sink. But buoyancy was not as obvious in the air, especially since the Montgolfiers believed that smoke provided the lift for their balloons.

THE BREAKTHROUGH

Although the Montgolfiers had not understood why their small balloons had risen in the air, they continued with their experiments. On June 5, 1783, they invited the public to witness the launching of their new invention. Their 39-foot balloon was made from pieces of linen that were buttoned together and then lined with paper to keep the hot air from seeping out. Attached to the balloon's neck was a container that held the smoke-producing fire. According to one account, the balloon rose to a height of 6,000 feet and flew about one and one-half miles from where the brothers had launched it.

Following their experiment, an official report of this first successful balloon launching was sent to the Académie des Sciences (National Academy of the Sciences) in Paris. The brothers were promptly invited to exhibit their invention in Paris, the country's center of government, science, and culture, but Joseph declined, saying he did not care for the high society of Paris. So Étienne went there alone, and alone he would change the way his fellow citizens—and all of Europe—would view the world.

The news of the Montgolfiers' success inspired the academy to commission further study of lighter-than-air flight, and a young physicist, Professor Jacques Alexandre César Charles, was selected to head the study. Professor Charles decided to work with hydrogen, a gas that had been discovered in 1766 by Henry Cavendish of England. Based on the reports of the Montgolfiers' balloon flight of

Balloon flight is often referred to as **lighter-than-air flight** because balloons derive their lift from hot air and hydrogen, which are lighter than cool air.

News of the Montgolfiers' successful balloon flight prompted Jacques Alexandre César Charles (1746-1823) to conduct his own lighter-than-air experiments. Unlike the Montgolfiers, however, Charles chose hydrogen to provide the lift for his balloon.

June 5, Charles concluded that hydrogen would be much lighter than the mysterious "Montgolfier's gas," which was simply heated and thinned air. Therefore, he realized that a much smaller balloon full of the extremely light (and extremely flammable) hydrogen could lift the same weight as a much larger hot-air balloon. The Montgolfier brothers had, in fact, tried to use hydrogen in their earlier experiments, but they had found the gas too difficult to hold in their small silk bags.

The problem of containing hydrogen challenged Charles as well. But he found a solution in an

hydrogen: a highly flammable gas that has one-fourteenth the density of air. First isolated in 1766 by Henry Cavendish, hydrogen is the most abundant element in the universe.

invention of brothers Marie-Noël and Jean Robert, who had developed a method of coating silk with a rubber varnish. The Roberts' treated silk proved to be the material that Charles needed for his experiment to succeed.

On the afternoon of August 27, 1783, Charles tested his first hydrogen balloon, the *Globe*. Filling his rather small 13-foot balloon with 943 cubic feet of hydrogen posed problems, not the least of which was preventing the highly flammable gas from exploding when the excited Parisian spectators had surged toward the balloon carrying torchlights on the evening before the test. But, despite a heavy rain, the balloon was successfully launched from the Champs-de-Mars (which would later be the site of the Eiffel Tower) in the center of Paris. The balloon quickly rose into the low clouds and vanished. Charles had demonstrated the power of hydrogen.

To ease the fears of the people who might see the balloon in the sky or watch it fall, the government had made the following announcement:

> Any one who shall see in the sky such a globe, which resembles the moon in eclipse, should be aware that, far from being an alarming phenomenon, it is only a machine that cannot possibly cause any harm, and which will some day prove useful to the wants of society.

Not everyone received this warning, however. When the balloon landed in the town of Gonesse some 15 miles away, a crowd of frightened peasants attacked it with pitchforks.

American statesman, inventor, and philosopher Benjamin Franklin (1725-1802) avidly followed the race to launch a balloon. He was in the crowd that witnessed the ascent of Charles's balloon on August 27, 1783.

While Charles went to work on a new balloon, the Montgolfier brothers took another major step forward and upward. On September 19, 1783, with King Louis XVI and Marie Antoinette in attendance, a 41-foot Montgolfier balloon, similar to the one that had been launched in June, took off from the grounds of the magnificent royal palace at Versailles. Attached to the bottom of the balloon was a simple cage that contained the first airborne travelers in history: a sheep, a duck, and a rooster.

The balloon carried its passengers to a height of 1,450 feet and traveled two miles in eight minutes before landing in the Forêt de (forest of) Vaucresson.

Thinking the devil was raining down evil upon them, the peasants of Gonesse tied the limp gasbag to the tail of a horse and sent the animal galloping down a country road, reducing the world's first gas balloon to shreds.

The rooster suffered an injured wing, apparently because it was kicked by the frightened sheep after landing. One can easily imagine the terror of the unsuspecting people on the ground when they saw the strange contraption floating above them and heard the bleating and quacking and crowing of the animals in the bobbing cage!

Once the brothers had demonstrated that hot-air-balloon flight was safe for animals, the next step was to send up humans in a balloon. The king of France suggested that the first humans to risk their lives in a free-flying balloon should be convicts awaiting execution. A 26-year-old medical doctor named François Pilâtre de Rozier disagreed. He believed that the Montgolfier brothers should bestow this historic honor upon a person of better character, such as himself. When Louis XVI agreed, the Montgolfiers' plans went forward. Before allowing a free flight, Étienne asked Rozier to go aloft in the balloon while it was attached to the ground with ropes. So his October 15, 1783, flight in a 49-foot fabric balloon was limited to 84 feet—the length of the rope—but he stayed airborne for four and one-half minutes and returned to the ground unharmed.

This experiment was proof enough that the Montgolfier balloons were safe. On November 21, 1783, in the Chateau de la Muette Gardens in the Bois de Boulogne, a huge park on the west side of Paris, the 49-foot balloon was ready for launching. It was grandly ornate, emblazoned with emblems of French royalty and the zodiac in gold on a blue background. In the ringed walkway below stood François

A patron of many early balloonists, Louis XVI (1754-1793) kept in his personal zoo the sheep that had "pioneered" balloon flight.

François Pilâtre de Rozier, here demonstrating the flammability of hydrogen, had pleaded with the king of France for permission to be the first to fly.

Pilâtre de Rozier and another passenger, François Laurent, the marquis d'Arlandes.

At just before two in the afternoon, with its container of burning straw and wool pouring smoke and hot air up into the balloon, the spectacular blue-and-gold sphere lifted off, leaving a trail of black smoke behind. Once in the air, the great balloon simply drifted back and forth over Paris with the winds. Watched by tens of thousands of fascinated Parisians, the two men climbed to 1,500 feet. At one point during the flight, they extinguished a small fire in the fabric of the balloon with a sponge and water that they had brought along for emergency use.

After 25 minutes in the air, the two adventurers landed on the Butte-aux-Cailles, almost six miles from where they had lifted off. Rozier and Laurent had crossed Paris in the air and returned safely to the ground. No longer was the sky foreign territory. In a very limited way, Joseph and Étienne Montgolfier, François Pilâtre de Rozier, and the marquis d'Arlandes had conquered the blue expanse above them.

Despite their triumph, the Montgolfiers still did not know how smoke could lift a device that weighed at least 1,000 pounds with passengers on board. Some historians claim the brothers believed the more foul smelling the smoke, the greater the lift, so they often burned old shoes and rotten meat to create a malodorous smoke. But the brothers were not hampered by their lack of knowledge. For them, it was enough that their balloons had flown.

Jacques Charles, however, did understand that hydrogen had made his balloon lift into the air. And on December 1, 1783, Professor Charles, along with Marie-Noël Robert—one of the brothers who had developed the rubber coating that had made Charles's balloon workable—took the first human flight in a hydrogen-filled balloon. They brought along an assortment of wines and champagne and a blanket to protect them from the cold. In full view of over 400,000 people, they lifted off from the Tuileries Gardens in Paris. Drifting with the wind, they traveled 27 miles to the small town of Nesle.

Ballast (often water or sand) can be thrown overboard to increase altitude in lighter-than-air flight. Letting hot air or hydrogen out of the balloon will decrease altitude.

Jacques Charles set a precedent for future exhibition flights by attempting to charge admission when he and Marie-Noël Robert became the first humans to fly in a hydrogen balloon on December 1, 1783.

Fearing they had insufficient lift to complete their flight across the English Channel, Jean Pierre Blanchard (above) and Dr. John Jeffries jettisoned everything possible, including their life-jackets and their clothing (except their underwear). Seeing that they were still going to crash, Blanchard and Jeffries urinated into rubber bags. They threw what they estimated was five or six pounds of urine overboard, which slowed their descent and allowed them to land safely in France.

THE RESULT

The next step in the conquest of the skies was to travel to a specific destination. On January 7, 1785, Jean Pierre Blanchard, a Frenchman, and Dr. John Jeffries, an American physician from Boston, took off in a hydrogen-filled balloon from Dover on the southeast coast of England, heading east. Two and one-half hours later, after flying 26 miles across the English Channel, they landed in the Forêt de Felmores near Calais, France.

The two aviators had made the first international journey by air, easily crossing the barrier that had protected England from invasion for hundreds of years. This achievement would profoundly affect Europe and the rest of the world in years to come.

Despite their success, a serious problem remained. A balloon could go only where the winds took it. Sometimes the wind blew in the direction a balloonist wanted to go; other times it did not. If the wind was not blowing in the proper direction, no balloonist, however experienced, could get where he or she wanted to go. Therefore, unless an inventor could make balloons steerable and controllable, they would never be much more than novelties.

Because of the near impossibility of making a balloon go where its pilot wished, people flew the hydrogen balloon only for recreation and demonstrations. But tethered balloons, which were held to the ground by long ropes, were put to practical use. On June 26, 1794, the French army watched their Austrian opponents from tethered balloons at the

Battle of Fleurus. In the 1860s, during the American Civil War, Thaddeus Lowe used a balloon inflated with coal gas to float above the Confederate lines. From there, he could observe and report troop movements back to the commanders of the Union forces via telegraph. Later, for a short period in the nineteenth and early twentieth centuries, a powered, steerable balloon—the airship—found its place in aviation history. Though highly flammable, hydrogen balloons would dominate the ballooning world well into the twentieth century.

Hot-air balloons fell out of use for many years because their smoke-filled flights were limited by the amount of burning material they could carry. Not until the 1970s did they become truly popular. Using compact, powerful, and clean propane burners to keep the air hot, thousands of adventurous aeronauts have floated high in the sky in brightly colored balloons for recreation and competitions.

François Pilâtre de Rozier hoped to cross the English Channel in this combination hot-air and hydrogen balloon he had designed for the journey. Combining the two balloon types proved fatal when, on June 15, 1785, the balloon exploded in flight, killing Rozier.

CHAPTER TWO

Henri Giffard
and the Dirigible

In those heady months of 1783, the Montgolfier brothers and Jacques Charles had proved it was possible to rise above the earth, drift along for many minutes, and then land safely. But was this flying, or was it merely floating? Was this enough to end thousands of years of envying the birds, or was it only the first small step on a long journey toward mastering the skies?

If free-flying balloons were to become vehicles for traveling from one place to another, they had to be able to move into the wind and go where their pilots wished, not merely where the unpredictable winds blew them. The balloons would have to become airships—ships of the air.

To attain the goal of traveling in the air, the first problem to solve was thrust, or power. How could airships be powered so they would move forward even if the wind was blowing in the opposite direction? Early dreamers saw propellers as one

Frenchman Henri Giffard (1825-1882) drew on his knowledge of engineering and steam-engine technology to build and fly the first successful dirigible.

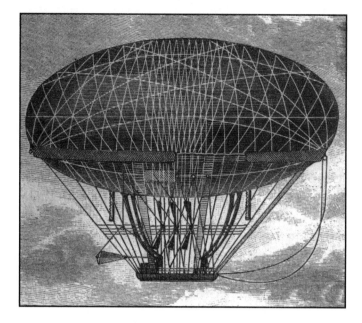

Jean-Baptiste Marie Meusnier created this advanced design for a dirigible in 1785—just two years after the Montgolfiers' balloon had first flown. Unfortunately, Meusnier was killed in battle before he ever had the chance to construct his dirigible.

Thomas Mackintosh published a far-fetched idea for a dirigible in 1835. He planned to tether a large number of birds to the vessel and then let them flap their way into history. Some reported Mackintosh had said that eagles could do the job, but that he would settle for strong pigeons if eagles proved to be untrainable.

promising way to move balloons forward, but such a propeller would have to be quite large. Even more daunting was the question of how it would be powered. Here, airship designers ran into the same problem that many years later would delay the invention of the airplane: they lacked a lightweight, powerful engine.

In 1850, Frenchman Pierre Jullien built and demonstrated a model airship that was powered by a clocklike mechanism. This small, streamlined ship was a successful model, and, although it was too small to carry human passengers, it provided useful information about how to design and propel an airship. It remained clear, however, that a power source greater than harnessed birds, human muscle, or clockwork mechanisms would be required to propel an airship capable of carrying humans through the sky. So, with the development of the internal-combustion gasoline engine still several decades away and electricity still in its infancy, the steam engine would have to power the airship.

Frenchman Henri Giffard would be the first person to apply steam-engine technology successfully to airships. Giffard worked professionally as a mechanical engineer and was known for his steam engine designs. In the 1840s, Giffard and a Dr. Le Berrier had built a small steam-powered model airship. This moderately successful experiment, as well as Pierre Jullien's clockwork experiments in 1850, would inspire Giffard to construct his own full-size, steam-powered dirigible. Giffard designed and built

James Watt patented his steam engine in 1769, giving rise to the Industrial Revolution. While steam engines proved to be very efficient in powering trains and steamships, as well as machines in the new factories, they were simply too heavy to power a craft that would travel in the air.

A balloon that one can steer is called an **airship** or a **dirigible**, which comes from the Latin word *dirigere*, meaning to direct or steer.

gondola: a basket or enclosure suspended beneath a balloon or dirigible to hold cargo or passengers

a dirigible dominated by a gasbag that was shaped like a thin football with pointed ends. It was 144 feet long and 39 feet in diameter, and it held almost 90,000 cubic feet of hydrogen. Mounted under the gasbag was the platform, or gondola, which held a steam engine, a propeller, and, of course, Giffard.

The steam engine was Giffard's great contribution to the progress of flight because it was a much more sensible source of power than anything previously tried or even proposed. Still, the engine only produced three horsepower (hp) while weighing 350 pounds, not including the 130 pounds of water and coke (a fuel processed from coal) that were required to fuel it. The coke was burned to turn water into

When he first isolated hydrogen in 1766, Henry Cavendish (1731-1810), shown here, used the words "inflammable air" to describe his discovery. Twenty years later, the French chemist Antoine Lavoisier (1743-1794) named the element hydrogen.

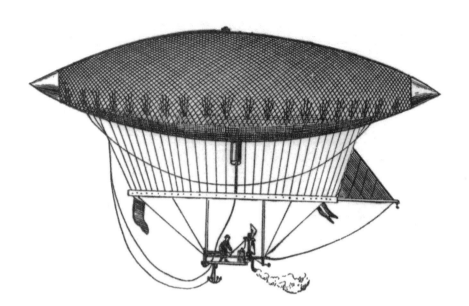

steam, and the steam engine was connected to an 11-foot propeller that drove the dirigible forward.

Giffard's second major contribution to aerial progress was his concern for safety—a rare quality at a time when other inventors appeared to rely more on faith to bring them through potentially dangerous experiences unharmed. The distance between his balloon and its gondola was about 20 feet, which reduced the chances of a spark from the steam boiler touching off a hydrogen explosion that could destroy the gasbag and kill the pilot. In addition, Giffard pointed the chimney for the exhaust downward, away from the huge envelope filled with hydrogen. He understood how dangerous a hydrogen explosion could be. Since Rozier's death in 1785—the first recorded aerial fatality—countless aeronauts had lost their lives as the result of carelessness.

Because he did not want to risk his life unnecessarily in his 1852 attempt to fly the first workable dirigible, Henri Giffard designed a downward-pointing chimney and hung the gondola some 20 feet below the hydrogen-filled gasbag.

THE BREAKTHROUGH

On September 24, 1852, Giffard began his flight at the Hippodrome (a horse-racing track) near the Arc de Triomphe in Paris. The three-hour flight, at about five miles per hour (mph), ended near Trappes, almost 17 miles southwest of the city. Throughout the journey, the steam engine hissed away, leaving a trail of steam and smoke behind it.

Giffard's trip was quite a feat. Dressed in a top hat and frock coat, Giffard had traveled more or less in a straight line, and he landed in one piece. Although his 3 hp airship had little operating power and was inherently clumsy, it had done its job.

Several more flights followed. During a later flight, Giffard flew in circles while steering the craft with a triangular cloth rudder.

Giffard dreamed of flying airships in all sorts of weather and in any kind of wind condition. But to do that, he needed a larger, more powerful airship. In 1855, Giffard built a second airship. This craft was almost 100 feet longer than the first, and it had an increased hydrogen capacity. But because Giffard had used the same engine, most historians cannot understand why he thought his second dirigible would fly any better than his first one.

Giffard asked a friend to accompany him on the test flight of his second airship. At the start of the flight, gas began to leak from the gasbag, which then became contorted. Suddenly, the airship pointed its nose upward. When some of the lines that connected the gasbag to the gondola broke, the balloon lurched free and quickly burst. Fortunately, Giffard and his passenger were only bruised in their fall to the ground, but the airship was a total loss. While that accident seems to have been the last of Giffard's hands-on dirigible experiments, it was not the end of his dreaming of the skies.

Giffard next began building large, passenger-carrying hydrogen balloons. By exposing as many people as possible to the experience, he hoped to interest the public in air travel. He created a sensation at the 1867 Paris Exhibition by selling tickets for brief rides in his tethered balloon. For the first time in history, anyone who was willing to pay could rise a few hundred feet above the earth and see Paris from the air. More than a decade later at the 1878 Paris Exhibition, Giffard's balloon carried an estimated 35,000 people aloft in tethered flights. But his balloons were not moving Giffard toward his ultimate goal of achieving practical dirigible flight. Although Giffard continued to work on better engines—steam-powered and otherwise—he never again experienced powered flight. Others who followed him would accomplish that goal.

One airship enthusiast who had been inspired by Giffard's success with steam engines was Camille Vert. In 1860, Vert had designed a surprisingly modern-looking dirigible that was shaped like a streamlined football with a rigid rudder at the rear. A closed gondola with a propeller at both ends was attached below, and the airship had wheels for take-off and landing. But the machine could not achieve flight.

In 1835, the comte de Lennox built the *Eagle,* a cigar-shaped airship that he displayed in London. This craft had four large paddles on either side that "experimental sailors" were to turn back and forth like the oars of ancient ships. No evidence exists that Lennox tried to fly his invention, nor is there any reason to think it would have worked if he had tried.

Even after Giffard had demonstrated his workable steam-powered dirigible in 1852, inventors such as Dupuy-de-Lôme continued to build human-powered machines that required large crews.

The next experimental airships used other types of power. In 1872, Dupuy-de-Lôme, a French naval engineer, built a dirigible that was designed to carry 14 people, 8 of whom were to turn a huge 30-foot propeller by hand. His airship made only a single short flight at a speed of five miles per hour. That same year in Germany, Paul Hänlein built an airship with an internal-combustion engine fueled with coal gas drawn from the gasbag. It made only a few short, tethered flights.

Next, in 1883, French brothers Albert and Gaston Tissandier used yet another means of propulsion: an electric motor. Together, the motor and the 24 batteries it needed to operate weighed 440 pounds and produced a mere 1.5 hp. Their airship suffered the same fate as all the other underpowered dirigibles. Although it was able to fly forward slowly, the craft could not effectively be controlled because it was so ungainly.

The first fully controllable dirigible was also powered by electricity. French army officers Charles Renard and A. C. Krebs built *La France*, a 165-foot dirigible with a 9 hp electric motor. On August 9, 1884, *La France* flew a five-mile circular course in 23 minutes, averaging a blazing 14.5 mph—the fastest anyone had ever traveled through the air.

With human and steam power showing no signs of having a future in flight, and electricity faring only a little better, the main obstacle to better flight still remained the lack of a small, light, powerful engine. Even the best of electric motors required a mass of heavy batteries that the aviator had to

Weighted down with 24 heavy batteries, French brothers Albert and Gaston Tissandier were able to fly their underpowered dirigible, but they did not fly fast enough to be satisfied with the results.

recharge frequently. The solution finally arrived in Germany with Gottlieb Daimler's 1885 invention of the gasoline-powered internal-combustion engine that would also power the first automobile.

Within a few years, those who had dreamed of conquering the skies were developing airships powered by internal-combustion engines. A fellow German, Dr. Karl Wölfert, built a small dirigible with a 2 hp, one-cylinder Daimler engine. Wölfert took the dirigible on its first flight on August 12, 1888, and he continued to test his machine over the years until 1897. That year, a flame from his engine came into contact with hydrogen from the balloon, causing an explosion that sent Wölfert and his mechanic plummeting to their deaths.

It was Alberto Santos-Dumont, the son of a wealthy Brazilian coffee plantation owner, who finally accomplished what Henri Giffard and many others had been trying to do for more than 50 years. Santos-Dumont built a powered, lighter-than-air craft that pilots could fly more or less where and when they wished.

Starting in 1898 with his airship *Number 1*, Santos-Dumont designed and built—and crashed and rebuilt—a series of one-person airships that worked. In 1901, he flew his *Number 6* with a 12 hp engine around the Eiffel Tower in Paris at 15 mph.

Brazilian Alberto Santos-Dumont (pictured here in his Number 9*), was the toast of Paris with his dirigibles that he flew from café to café. In 1906, he became the first human to make a powered, controlled airplane flight in Europe.*

THE RESULT

The efforts to develop airships had a significant impact on the future of aviation. In the early 1900s, Count Ferdinand von Zeppelin built the first of many huge dirigibles, which would soon be called zeppelins. During World War I (1914-1918), German engineers filled the zeppelins with hydrogen gas and used them to drop bombs on England, raining terror from the skies on the people below.

After the war, dirigibles became the first long-range airliners, carrying passengers in luxury and comfort on flights around Europe and later across the Atlantic Ocean to North and South America.

Count Ferdinand von Zeppelin's first large dirigible, the LZ-1, made its initial ascent on July 2, 1900. Although this airship lacked adequate control and power, Zeppelin's later airships were so successful that the name "Zeppelin" came to mean airship.

Originally designed to be filled with nonflammable helium, the Hindenburg *had to rely on cheaper, more easily attained hydrogen for lifting power. This spelled a violent end for the zeppelin when, on May 6, 1937, a spark ignited the hydrogen, causing a huge explosion.*

However, a string of serious accidents caused by bad weather and mechanical problems raised doubts about the future of the dirigible. The use of dirigibles for passenger travel ended abruptly on May 6, 1937, when a German zeppelin, the *Hindenburg*, crashed in flames at Lakehurst, New Jersey.

The magnificent 803-foot *Hindenburg*, which could cruise at 81 mph and carry as many as 200 passengers, was powered by four 1,000 hp airplane

engines. Because the United States had refused to sell nonexplosive helium to Nazi Germany, the mechanics had filled the zeppelin with 7 million cubic feet of highly flammable hydrogen. On the May 6 flight, a spark, perhaps caused by static, made the hydrogen erupt into flames. In a few seconds, all was over for the dirigible. Miraculously, of the 97 people on board, 62 survived the crash.

Despite this horrible accident, the military, especially the U.S. Navy (which had access to the nonexplosive helium), continued to use dirigibles effectively to patrol for submarines during and after World War II. And for decades, the Goodyear Company has used blimps to fly ads and TV cameras overhead at outdoor sporting events. But because airplanes can carry many more people faster and more safely, there is little chance that airships will ever again be used for passengers.

Even at its height of popularity, airship travel was nothing like bird flight. Airships were large and slow and terribly clumsy, and they were easily blown around by high winds. If humans were to fly, they would have to do so with wings, not with bags filled with gas.

Henri Giffard died in 1882 at age 57 without ever achieving his goal of building a truly practical airship. He did, however, design, build, and fly the first aerial vehicle that could be controlled by a pilot while in flight. Giffard, whom historians often call the "father of the airship," can, therefore, be given credit for one of the major steps in the evolution of aviation.

Zeppelins and blimps are both dirigibles, airships that are powered and can be steered or controlled. A **zeppelin** is generally rigid with an internal frame; a **blimp** is generally non- or semi-rigid.

CHAPTER THREE

Otto Lilienthal and the Glider

Birds do not have to design and build their wings and then spend years inventing an engine so that they can use them. Humans who wished to imitate birds, however, had to resolve every problem on the way to flight, designing and trying out the span, area, and curvature of wings in a variety of ways until they arrived at a workable combination. The assumption among the early innovators that studying all manner of birds was the way to learn how to design an airplane had led many would-be flyers astray. But it had taught them one crucial concept: they learned that a wing must be curved from front to back so the reduced air pressure on top of the wing would produce a lifting force.

The first person to understand lifting force was George Cayley, an English scientist who published scientific papers on the subject as early as 1809. Too many would-be airplane designers ignored his work—even after Cayley built a glider

Otto Lilienthal (1848-1896) studied the flight of birds for many years before building and flying the world's first successful gliders.

heavier-than-air flight refers to flight in which lift is derived from wings, as on an airplane, in contrast to lighter-than-air flight, where lift is provided by gas or hot air, which is lighter than regular air.

that, according to his notes, flew down a hill with a young boy on board.

The first person to make repeated tests of a heavier-than-air flying machine was Frenchman François Letur. In 1853, he built a combination glider/parachute that carried him from a balloon safely to the ground, but he died while attempting a similar flight the next year. Three years after Letur's death, Jean-Marie Le Bris, a French naval officer, built a glider shaped like an albatross, a bird he had studied while at sea. After a few brief successful flights, he crashed and broke his leg, ending his experiments with flying machines.

The flying career of the first major figure in the development of the airplane began in 1861, when 13-year-old Otto Lilienthal started experimenting with homemade wings in his hometown of Anklam, now in Germany. Working with his brother Gustav, Otto carefully recorded the results of every test, no matter how unsuccessful. The two spent many hours observing the large storks that would circle above for several minutes without flapping their wings.

The Lilienthal brothers noticed that the shy birds always ran into the wind to take off, even when danger lurked in that direction. Soon, Otto and Gustav began to sense the importance of wind speed. From thin strips of beech wood, the two built a set of wings. Then they tried to take off down a hill by flapping the wings like the storks had done.

After two summers of youthful experimenting, the brothers realized that they lacked adequate power with only their arms flapping the artificial wings. Otto and Gustav added a pumping lever to utilize their leg power as well, but they still could not get off the ground. Their next step was to build wings that more closely resembled those of a bird— wings that would spread open on the downstroke to catch more air. But the lack of money and family support slowed their activities, and Gustav eventually lost interest in further experimentation.

In 1867, Otto began to study engineering at the Berlin Trade Academy and found his mechanical studies applicable to his interest in flight. Then, in 1870, he went to fight for Prussia in the Franco-Prussian war against France. After Prussia's victory the following year, Otto returned to his home and found work as an engineer.

Fanciful designs for ornithopters often revealed the creative abilities of humans. Rarely, however, did they demonstrate that humans could fly.

Lilienthal then began to conduct basic research on bird flight. This led to designing and constructing several small mechanical birds, powered by coiled springs. Next, he built a larger, stork-sized model with wings that, through a series of levers and rods, were powered by a miniature steam engine.

Although progress was slow, Lilienthal learned a little with each step. He increasingly became convinced that all of the work being done on airships was a waste of time and that only an airplane—powered by either propellers or flapping wings—would produce the controlled, extended flight that everyone

This fifteenth-century ornithopter design by Leonardo da Vinci included a rudder-control system that the pilot could operate with straps and harnesses by moving his head.

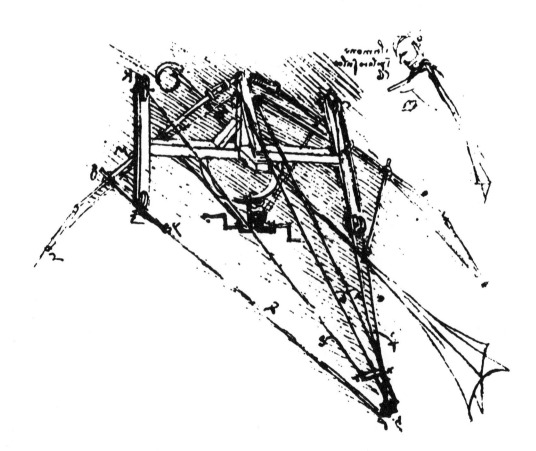

was seeking. During the summer of 1873, when he recognized that one of the secrets to the stork's easy flight was the curvature of its wings, he set up a machine with two rotating arms. On each arm, he attached test wings of varied shapes. By whirling the arms around, Lilienthal discovered that the shapes most resembling a stork's had the greatest lifting force and the least wind resistance. He also realized that the speed of the air flowing over the wings played a major role in lifting them.

After nearly three decades of analyzing the construction of bird wings and their motion at take-off, in flight, and on landing, Lilienthal had gained a unique understanding of the most successful flyers: birds. By 1889, Lilienthal's studies culminated in the publication of one of the great works about the science of flight, *Birdflight as the Basis of Aviation.*

Among Lilienthal's great concerns was the amount of attention being paid to lighter-than-air flying machines and the discouraging attitude of most scientists toward heavier-than-air flight. In fact, Lilienthal complained to a writer for *McClure's* magazine in 1894 that a special commission of experts organized by the German government had "laid it down as a fundamental principle, once and for all, that it was *impossible* for a man to fly." Lilienthal pointed out that balloons had "nothing in common with the birds." He had a goal—to fly—and it would take more than a panel of "experts" to keep him from doing it.

It is . . . [birds] that we must take as our model and exemplar. What we are seeking is the means of free motion in the air, in any direction. In this the balloon is of no aid.
—Otto Lilienthal

THE BREAKTHROUGH

Just as a young bird takes to the air in short steps before flying freely, Otto Lilienthal proceeded cautiously. In 1891, he built a 40-pound glider with 23-foot wings made of muslin soaked in wax and stretched over a wooden frame of split willow. His first attempt to pilot the craft from a height of 19 feet produced a glide of only 16 feet in a strong wind. But this short hop was just the beginning.

Gradually, Lilienthal learned how to adjust his glider and predict its reaction to the forces of nature. He was eventually able to glide 114 feet down the gently sloping hill.

Hanging freely below his biplane glider, Otto Lilienthal could control his craft in the air by swinging his body weight.

Otto Lilienthal's next glider was larger. It weighed 53 pounds, and its wings were 175 square feet in area. In this craft, he was able to glide farther than 250 feet at speeds up to 16 mph. Lilienthal had created the first successful hang glider, and now he began to manufacture and sell them to prospective pilots throughout Europe.

Up to this point, Lilienthal had controlled his flight by shifting his weight to make the glider rise or fall and veer to the left or to the right. But now he set out to develop controls. Although Lilienthal would continue to rely heavily on shifting his body to maintain stability, his new glider had levers that allowed him to change the shape of the wings during flight. Little by little, he was inventing the airplane.

Lilienthal had built his gliders as "schooling machines" to help him master the art of piloting a heavier-than-air craft. Thus, he would be prepared for actual powered flight once he had perfected his flapping-winged ornithopter. He was learning to glide, but he did not seem to be getting much closer to his real goal of powered flight. And the difficulty of maintaining steady flight in strong or gusty winds made him increasingly envious of the birds that flew so effortlessly on the nearby hills.

To improve his flying ability, Lilienthal had his own 50-foot hill built in 1892 in the Berlin suburb of Lichterfelde with dirt from an excavated canal. This cone-shaped mound was better suited to his experiments than any natural hill because he didn't have to rely on a certain wind direction to take off successfully. If the wind was blowing from the south, he

It was only after Lilienthal had shown that such an adventure was feasible that courage was gathered to experiment with full-sized machines carrying a man through the air.
—Octave Chanute

could jump into the wind—as the storks had—and fly in that direction because the cone-shaped mound provided a downhill slope in every direction. If the wind was blowing from the north on the next day, he could take off into the north and glide down that side of the slope.

In 1894, Lilienthal was photographed gliding from his hill in Lichterfelde. Said to be the first photographs ever taken of a human being in flight, the photos showed the various stages from takeoff to landing and proved to the world that a glider had lifted a human being into the sky. Publications carrying these photos would inspire many other aviation enthusiasts, including Orville and Wilbur Wright, to take action and attempt to fly.

Despite his growing knowledge of the science of flight, Lilienthal still believed that flapping wings

Pulling back his legs, Lilienthal prepares to land at the base of the hill he had constructed for his gliding experiments.

and a motor would provide the thrust that was needed to achieve his ultimate goal of powered flight. So, throughout 1895 and into 1896, he worked on a flapping-winged ornithopter, which was powered by a small carbonic-acid engine of his own design. Initial tests showed that the flapping wings did not seem to improve the craft's performance, but Lilienthal was undeterred. He worked on his machine even as he continued to conduct unpowered gliding experiments.

During this period, Lilienthal found some hills near the German town of Stöllen where he could make exceptional glides. On Sunday, August 9, 1896, he went there for a day of flight tests. The weather was pleasant, although perhaps not ideal for gliding, as the wind blew at a mere 10 mph.

That day, what began as a seemingly standard glide ended when a sudden gust of wind took Lilienthal by surprise. His glider's nose rose too far and too quickly, and the wings stalled and lost all their lift. Because he was no more than 50 feet above the ground, Lilienthal had no chance to recover from the inevitable dive and was paralyzed from a broken back in the crash. He died the following afternoon.

Although gasoline-powered internal-combustion engines were available and proven at the time, Lilienthal designed his own engine. It was driven by carbonic acid that was compressed in a cylinder.

THE RESULT

Despite Lilienthal's erroneous beliefs about flapping-winged devices, his contributions to the eventual accomplishment of powered, heavier-than-air flight were great. Considering the problem of flight, he studied birds and their wings and built gliders based on his findings. Then he practiced gliding and made adjustments to his gliders based on what he had learned in flight. By using this scientific method of observation and application, he set the stage for the next clear thinkers in aviation—the Wright brothers.

While Lilienthal's achievements were valuable during the years immediately following his death, his invention of the hang glider would grow in

Although the Wright brothers found inspiration in Lilienthal's work and based some of their early gliders on his calculations, they never built a machine in which the pilot would dangle below the wings and shift his weight for control.

importance many decades later. In the early 1970s, thousands of people took up hang-gliding, creating a new kind of "aerial surfing." Hang gliders became more aeronautically advanced, and rapid improvements in materials and wing designs produced some amazing performances. After being towed to high altitudes behind airplanes, more recent hang-glider flights have lasted almost eight hours and exceeded a distance of 300 miles.

This new interest in gliding no doubt would have pleased Lilienthal, for he saw gliders not only as research tools, but also as sporting vehicles. He sold them to people who simply wanted to experience the thrill of flying.

As long as people fly and glide, Otto Lilienthal will be remembered. Grateful enthusiasts have built memorials to the inventor in the southwest section of Berlin and in his hometown of Anklam, Germany. At least eight original Lilienthal gliders are still in existence, including an 1894 model that is displayed in the Smithsonian Institution in Washington, D.C. Today, whenever a flyer risks his or her life, many will recall Lilienthal's final words, "Sacrifices must be made."

Octave Chanute (1832-1910), another early would-be aviator, built the first bridge across the Missouri River and gained a strong reputation as civil engineer before devoting himself to the field of aviation. A frequent visitor to the Wright camp at Kitty Hawk in the 1900s, Chanute also traveled to Germany to observe Lilienthal in action and conducted his own gliding experiments on the sand dunes of Lake Michigan in the 1890s.

CHAPTER 4

Samuel Pierpont Langley and the *Aerodrome*

Early in the nineteenth century, Sir George Cayley spoke of the wonders of flight:

> I feel perfectly confident . . . that this noble art of flying will soon be brought home to man's general convenience, and that we shall be able to transport ourselves and families, and their goods and chattels, more securely by air than by water, and with a velocity of from 20 to 100 miles per hour. To produce this effect it is only necessary to have a first mover, which will generate more power in a given time, in proportion to its weight, than the animal system of muscles.

This brilliant Englishman's thinking was far ahead of anyone else's, but he was too optimistic about the possibility of turning his ideas into a blueprint for flight. Almost 100 years would pass before Cayley's theories would finally become reality. One of the innovators who would make this possible was scientist and inventor Samuel Pierpont Langley.

Although he never went to college, Samuel Pierpont Langley (1834-1906) was able to rise to the position of secretary of the Smithsonian Institution, the prestigious scientific organization in Washington, D.C.

Englishman George Cayley (1773-1857) was among the first to propose driving an airplane forward with a propeller. To power the propeller, he suggested an "explosion machine" more than 50 years before the development of the internal-combustion gasoline engine.

In the hope that his ideas for flight would not be lost and forgotten, Cayley scratched this design for a fixed-wing aircraft on a silver disc in 1799.

In the very early days of flight, experimenters primarily considered three basic ways of getting off the ground: balloons, ornithopters, and helicopters. Balloons were simple, and they worked, but only in a very limited way. Ornithopters, modeled after birds, seemed the most obvious flying machine, but no one could perfect them. And it was still far too difficult to create a working model of a helicopter.

While most would-be flyers were trying techniques that would take many decades to develop, others were working on yet a fourth idea: a fixed-wing, engine-driven airplane. That craft, too, took a long time to get off the ground, but it would eventually turn out to be the best of all the flying machines dreamed up over the years.

The first person to consider such a design was George Cayley, a little-known British student of flight. As early as 1799, shortly after George Washington, the first president of the United States, had left office, Cayley realized that a properly shaped wing was the secret to constructing an airplane that would fly successfully.

Cayley, who is now known as the "Father of Aerial Navigation," had etched his proposed design onto a small silver disc that is at the Science Museum in London, England. On one side of the disc is a diagram of the forces that affect an airplane in flight. On the other side, Cayley etched a simple airplane with a single wing, a tail in back, and a fuselage containing a cockpit for the pilot.

In 1809 and 1810, Cayley published the world's first article about heavier-than-air flight, "On Aerial

Navigation," which described the principles of aero-dynamics and their practical application. Although nothing of the sort yet existed, Cayley even suggested using an internal-combustion engine to drive the airplane forward.

At about the same time, Cayley also built a five-foot glider—probably the first such craft ever constructed. He made other, larger gliders and in the 1850s eventually built one large enough to carry a human. This machine reportedly glided down a hill, piloted by Cayley's coachman. The unhappy coachman promptly quit, stating he had been hired to drive horses, not to fly!

Although none of his gliders had any sort of engine, Cayley had formulated an idea and tested it with positive results. The lack of a lightweight and powerful engine remained the most obvious problem faced by everyone who was trying to invent a powered flying machine. Springs or tightly wound elastic could power model planes, but an engine with enough power to lift several hundred pounds—the combined weight of a pilot and the machine—simply did not exist. So inventors had to continue to test their ideas on small model airplanes.

The first man to take Cayley's work seriously and carry it forward was a fellow Englishman named William Henson. Henson never constructed his 1842 design of the huge *Aerial Steam Carriage*, but his drawings, which greatly resembled a modern airplane, influenced and inspired other designers and would-be aviators. Color posters of the *Carriage's* 150-foot wings, broad tail, twin pusher propellers,

In 1843, William Henson attempted to finance the building of his modern-looking Aerial Steam Carriage *by selling stock in his Aerial Steam Transit Company.*

enclosed cabin, and tricycle landing gear show that William Henson was a true visionary among aviation theorists.

Although Henson and a colleague, John Stringfellow, were unable to complete a full-size version of Henson's design, they built a scale model with a 20-foot wingspan in 1847. Unfortunately, this machine failed to fly under the steam power that drove its propellers. Disheartened by the experience, Henson gave up on aviation and left England for a new life in the United States.

In 1848, John Stringfellow, now working alone, built a 10-foot scale model based on the original *Aerial Steam Carriage*, which he managed to fly with a miniature steam engine he had helped to develop. One flight that reportedly covered 120 feet—a stunning achievement at that time—somehow failed to attract attention or praise, and Stringfellow, too, left the aviation scene. Twenty years later, in 1868, he returned and displayed both a model airplane and a steam engine at the first Aeronautical Exhibition, held at London's Crystal Palace. Although the

John Stringfellow pressed on with the Aerial Steam Carriage *and built a scale model that was said to have flown 120 feet—as far as Orville Wright would fly in his first success at powered flight at Kitty Hawk.*

model plane barely flew, it stood out as an exceptional design, and Stringfellow's steam engine, designed for use in airplanes, earned him a prize of £100 ($9,000 by today's standards). Two decades after his initial unheralded experiments, Stringfellow saw a shift in public opinion. The world was slowly becoming interested in aviation.

Following Stringfellow, the next aviation visionary, Frenchman Alphonse Pénaud, built his first successful modern model airplane when he was only 21. With a wingspan of 20 inches and a pusher propeller (powered by a wound rubber band) behind

With its rubber-band-powered propeller, Alphonse Pénaud's model airplane was similar to the balsa-wood models that children fly today.

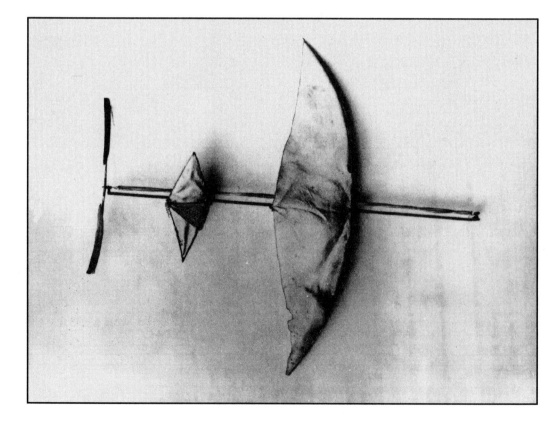

its tail, the model once flew 131 feet in 11 seconds. Pénaud's later designs incorporated an amazing number of modern ideas, including what is now the standard design for airplane tails and controls, an enclosed cockpit with windows, and full control by the pilot. But Pénaud, unfortunately, was never able to put any of these ideas into practice. In 1880, at the age of 29, he committed suicide.

In 1874, Felix du Temple of France built a fairly modern-looking monoplane with a steam-driven propeller in its nose. The machine never achieved true flight and was only able to accomplish a brief, uncontrolled hop down an inclined ramp.

A **monoplane** is an airplane with only one set of wings. A **biplane** is an airplane with two sets of main wings, one above the other.

While most inventors were concentrating on testing their ideas with models, a Russian set out to build the world's first large airplane. In 1884, Alexander Mozhaiski, an officer in the Imperial Russian Navy, produced a 2,000-pound, steam-powered monoplane with 75-foot wings. But because existing engines did not have enough power to get an airplane into the air and keep it there, Mozhaiski's monoplane merely bounced down an incline.

The next person to try his hand at inventing the airplane was Clement Ader, a Frenchman who built his *Eole* in 1890. Although the plane was less than half the size of Mozhaiski's machine, it was almost as powerful. Some people said it skimmed above the ground for 150 feet, but no records exist to support this claim.

In 1894, in England, Sir Hiram Maxim built what was the largest and most powerful airplane up to that time. His biplane was an outsized 25 feet in

Born in the United States, Sir Hiram Maxim (1840-1916) became a British subject in 1900 after living in Great Britain for many years. Before developing an interest in aviation, Maxim invented the water-cooled Maxim machine gun (1884) and was knighted for his contribution to the British military.

Hiram Maxim estimated that his giant biplane produced 10,000 pounds of lift when it broke through its safety track during the inventor's first and only attempt at flight.

height, and its wingspan was 104 feet. With two 180 hp steam engines and a three-person crew, this amazing contraption weighed some 8,000 pounds.

Maxim's biplane made one serious attempt to fly. On the last day of July in 1894, Maxim fired up the steam engines and headed down the safety track that he had designed to guide the plane. The huge machine lifted suddenly and broke through one of the track rails that was supposed to keep it under control. The crash badly damaged the airplane, and

Maxim gave up on the project. Perhaps he had been frightened by the crash, or perhaps he was frustrated at having spent so much money on his failed project.

Three years later, in 1897, Maxim's French rival, Clement Ader, was back in action. This time, he built the bat-shaped, twin-engine *Avion III* with two strange-looking propelle

cond

and t

secor

repor

was tl

the m

left th

by dre

ized t

Althou

to beli

their c

No less a genius than Leonardo da Vinci believed that the bat was the ideal model for human-carrying flying machines.

Frenchman Clement Ader spent more than $120,000 in his 25-year quest to build a workable flying machine.

aerodynamics: the science of air in motion and the motion of objects in air

and engines that would soon defy the skeptics. This progress would set the stage for the next innovator in the field of aviation, Samuel Pierpont Langley.

Born in Roxbury, Massachusetts, in 1834, Langley would rise to prominence in the field of astronomy before establishing his name in aviation. Even though he had only a high-school education, by the time he was 32 years old, he had become a professor of physics at the Western University of Pennsylvania (now the University of Pittsburgh), where he served as director of the Allegheny Observatory. Twenty-one years later, in 1887, Langley became the secretary of the Smithsonian Institution in Washington, D.C., and in that position directed of one of the world's most respected scientific organizations.

Langley's 1888 book, *The New Astronomy*, as well as his invention of the bolometer, a highly sensitive temperature meter, did much to advance both the field of astronomy and his reputation as a scientist. Langley's study of space led to an interest in flight. In 1891, he wrote *Experiments in Aerodynamics*. The simple fact that a respected scientist believed in the possibility of human flight would encourage many would-be flyers to press on with their own flight experiments.

THE BREAKTHROUGH

After building dozens of small model airplanes that were powered by rubber bands, Langley set out to build a larger, steam-powered model. On May 6, 1896, from a houseboat moored on the Potomac River, he launched his *Aerodrome #5* with a catapult device. Powered by only a 1 hp steam engine, the 14-foot craft flew for one and one-half minutes and 3,000 feet. After it landed gently on the water, Langley dried out the *Aerodrome #5* and launched it again.

Langley was satisfied with the results of his 1896 experiments and decided to let others carry on with further innovations involving human flight. But shortly after the start of the Spanish-American War in 1898, the War Department invited Langley—then in his mid-sixties and in ill health—to build an airplane that could be used in the war. With a budget of $50,000, Langley, against his doctor's advice, set out to put the U.S. military in the sky.

While Langley's crew was building the large *Aerodrome*, the war ended, and so did the government's interest in funding his invention of a plane. But Langley pressed on with his great experiment with financial support from the Smithsonian.

In August 1903, with the full-size *Aerodrome* almost finished, Langley flew his final model, a quarter-scale craft powered by a small gasoline-fueled piston engine. Its flight of about 1,000 feet at 30 mph was the first for any airplane equipped with the type of engine that eventually would make it possible for humans to take to the skies.

Writing for *McClure's* magazine in 1897, Langley stated that he felt he had accomplished his goal, "the demonstration of the practicability of mechanical flight." But, he wrote, "for the next stage, which is the commercial and practical development of the idea, it is probable that the world may look to others."

Like the full-size *Aerodrome*, the *#5* was a **tandem-winged** craft; that is, its two wings were arranged one behind the other, as on a dragonfly.

The term "aerodrome" that Samuel Langley used to describe his aircraft was actually the French word for flying field or airport.

piston engine: an internal-combustion engine in which small explosions push pistons back and forth within a cylinder to produce mechanical power

A board member of the Smithsonian Institution and inventor of the telephone, Alexander Graham Bell (1847-1922) was present at the first successful flight of the Aerodrome #5 on May 6, 1896.

radial engine: a piston engine with fixed cylinders arranged in a radial pattern like spokes on a wheel, as opposed to a "V" or an in-line pattern

Two months later, the *Aerodrome* was ready. Its two wings spanned 48 feet and had a total wing area of more than 1,000 square feet. Langley made a serious error in building the large *Aerodrome* as simply a scaled-up version of his earlier models—a mistake that almost definitely would have spelled doom if other problems had not wrecked the plane sooner. As he had done with the models, Langley hoped to launch his full-scale machine catapult-style from a houseboat. But because the *Aerodrome* had no landing gear of any sort, the pilot, standing in an open compartment at the lowest point of the machine, was certain to hit the water first.

Langley had made some (but not many) provisions for the pilot to maneuver the full-scale *Aerodrome*. To control climbing and diving, the aviator used one steering wheel that moved the tail up or down. A second wheel controlled a vertical rudder between the two wings, allowing the pilot to turn left or right. The pilot, however, could not make the airplane bank, or tilt to the side, while turning. To Langley, flying through the air was of primary interest; controlling the machine was only secondary.

The plane's engine, however, was a great advance. Stephen Balzer, an engineer from New York, had developed a water-cooled radial engine that Charles Manly, Langley's top assistant and pilot, further modified and even improved upon. It was no larger than the engine that would take the Wright brothers into the air at Kitty Hawk, but it produced four times as much power.

On October 7, 1903, with the Manly-Balzer engine installed and ready to drive the *Aerodrome's* two large propellers, Langley's assistants placed the aircraft on the catapult launching device on top of their specially built houseboat that was moored off the Virginia shore of the Potomac River. Manly climbed into the cockpit to await the launching.

The assistants started the engine, fired a sky-rocket to alert photographers on the nearby Virginia shore, and then set off another rocket as the catapult shot the machine forward. The *Aerodrome* headed down the sloping track, cleared the edge of the launching platform—and plopped into the river.

Langley's houseboat with a catapult launching device on top was ready for the October 7 demonstration flight.

We hope that Prof. Langley
will not put his substantial
greatness as a scientist to
further peril by continuing
to waste his time, and the
money involved, in further
airship experiments.
—The *New York Times*

One reporter who witnessed the failed attempt said it "simply slid into the water like a handful of mortar." Charles Manly managed to escape as the craft hit the river, and he was rescued a few minutes later.

While Langley explained the accident as a mechanical failure, perhaps related to the launching equipment, the press jumped with glee. Newspapers had long predicted failure for this and all other airplanes, and reporters were not shy in bragging about their foresight. The *New York Times* declared that at least a million years would pass before an airplane would carry humans across the skies.

Undaunted, Langley and his crew went back to work, repairing the airplane and the houseboat's launching catapult. They moored the houseboat closer to Washington, D.C., off Hains Point, where the Potomac and the Anacostia Rivers flow together. By December 8, everything was ready for the second attempt to send the *Aerodrome* into the sky, and Manly was prepared to risk his life in another flight. Night was coming on as the assistants triggered the catapult, and the machine hurtled forward.

This time, the *Aerodrome* tilted upward before slipping into the frigid water, tail first. Manly managed to free himself from the upside-down pilot's compartment, but he bumped his head against a piece of ice in his attempt to escape. Dazed, he scrambled to the surface of the icy river and was hauled aboard the houseboat, where the crew wrapped him in warm blankets.

While Manly was recovering, the workmen tried to lift the *Aerodrome* back on the boat. But in doing so, they damaged the airplane even more. Samuel Langley's machine was in ruins. Although he tried to blame the accident on another mechanical failure, photographs of the launching proved the craft had been structurally weak.

Langley's failure to understand the difference between a scale model and a full-scale airplane had caused the mishaps. Not realizing that for a full-scale airplane to work properly, some of the model's dimensions had to be changed more than others, he had mistakenly multiplied both the length and wingspan of the quarter-scale model by four.

Unfortunately, the Aerodrome collapsed as it left the launch pad and fell into the river. Langley and Charles Manly blamed the mishap on the launching apparatus and on the unskilled workmen who had been hired to assist them with the project.

Since the machines Langley built seemed to have such an affinity for the water, one journalist suggested that Langley should direct his efforts toward constructing a submarine!

THE RESULT

The December 8, 1903, mishap ended the *Aerodrome* project. Langley, suddenly the laughingstock of the national press, was finished with aviation. He still received full credit, however, for designing, building, and flying the largest and most successful *model* airplanes to date. History also credits him with flying the first large model airplane with a gasoline engine. And so Langley provides the link that connects the gliding experiments of Otto Lilienthal with the first powered, controlled flight of Orville Wright.

During a patent fight in 1914 between the Wright brothers and those accused of pirating their work, another pioneer aviator, Glenn Curtiss, attempted to prove that the Langley *Aerodrome* had been the first airplane capable of flying. He believed that if he could prove this, the Wrights would not be able to claim they had invented the airplane. After rebuilding the plane, Curtiss flew it several times in public. But he had modified it so extensively that the craft was really a new airplane. Curtiss proved little and returned the tandem-winged *Aerodrome* to the Smithsonian Institution.

Because of Langley's great influence at the Smithsonian, the institute displayed his *Aerodrome* as the first successful airplane in history. This upset the Wright brothers, who shipped their 1903 Wright *Flyer* to the Science Museum in London, where it stayed until 1946. Both airplanes are now at the Smithsonian, although the fully restored *Aerodrome* has been in storage for many years.

Despite his many accomplishments, the press relentlessly ridiculed Langley's failures. In 1906, he died from a stroke, a sad and humiliated man. After Langley's death, however, Wilbur Wright generously gave him credit and admitted that his *Aerodrome* experiments "had a great influence in determining my brother and myself to take up work in this science, and without doubt it similarly influenced others."

In 1914, seaplane innovator Glenn Curtiss rebuilt and successfully flew Langley's Aerodrome.

CHAPTER FIVE

The Wright Brothers and the Airplane

For most of the years in which humans were attempting to figure out how to fly, they built the machines of their dreams. If they dreamed about birds, they made mechanical birds. If they dreamed of whirling wings, they constructed machines with whirling blades that were supposed to lift them straight up. Inspired by their dreams, these visionaries would build a craft and then try to fly it, with little or no idea why they kept failing.

The reason for their failures was that hardly any of these inventions were truly scientific. That is, the would-be innovators did not theorize and test and then go back to the laboratory for more careful thinking about what had been successful and what had gone wrong with their experiments. While their contraptions may have enthusiastically flapped or rotated or whirled, only the machines that engineers designed and built with a knowledge of the laws of science stood any chance of flying.

Starting out in their bicycle workshop in Dayton, Ohio, Orville (left) and Wilbur Wright applied themselves tirelessly to the challenge of human flight.

In Germany, Otto Lilienthal tried to approach the challenge of flight as a way to test new ideas. He made plans for and then built simple machines. From his test flights, he learned something about how these machines worked and why they did not perform as well as he had hoped they would. Lilienthal remained convinced that he could turn his wonderful glider into some sort of powered aircraft. But he was killed in a crash before he could carry out further tests.

Being a scientist of considerable stature, Samuel Langley should have been the sort of person to attack the problems of flight in a highly methodical manner. His success with large, powered models suggests that his early work was indeed scientific. But his mistaken notion that he need only enlarge his models to create a successful airplane that could carry passengers spelled failure for him.

Scientists are not the only people who can employ the scientific method. In fact, two bicycle builders from Dayton, Ohio, were able to apply science to making airplanes. They moved ahead slowly and carefully, testing each new idea—no matter how insignificant it seemed—before moving on to the next. As they were inventing the airplane, they were also learning how to fly it.

Brothers Orville and Wilbur Wright of Dayton had the combination of skills and attitude that was necessary to turn their dreams into reality. The sons of a bishop in the United Brethren Church, Wilbur was born in 1867 and Orville in 1871. Though neither received a high school diploma, both Orville

and Wilbur read widely in their spare time, and the Wright home was a place where discussions of history, religion, and science were common.

The Wright brothers became printers in 1890, designing and building much of their own equipment. Orville also established a weekly newspaper, listing himself on the masthead as the publisher and his older brother as the editor. By 1892, they had established a bicycle shop in which they assembled, sold, and rented bicycles. For his own enjoyment and to advertise their business, Orville did some bicycle racing, using the best machines that he and his older brother could build.

Wilbur Wright, at left (1867-1912), and his younger brother, Orville (1871-1948), realized the importance of practice and safety in flying. They spent three years experimenting with unpowered gliders before they ever attempted a powered flight.

By the mid-1890s, the two brothers were seeking a new challenge. In 1896, the first automobile in Dayton got their attention, but it was not enough to interest them in the automobile business. Instead, their enthusiasm for flying grew. Orville and Wilbur learned that year of the work of Otto Lilienthal in Germany. When Lilienthal died only months later in a gliding accident, the Wright brothers became determined to meet the challenge of human flight. With their mechanical aptitude, they believed that they could build a better, safer flying machine.

Before beginning their own experiments, the Wright brothers—unlike many others who earlier had tried to fly—wanted to learn all they could about what other innovators had done before them. The

Otto Lilienthal's aviation experiments stimulated the Wrights' own pioneering efforts in flight.

few books and articles they found concentrated on bird flight. Seeing little future in flapping-winged ornithopters—and even less in balloons—the Wrights turned to gliders, hoping to develop them sufficiently to permit the kind of soaring they had observed in large birds. A successful glider would provide the foundation for their ultimate goal: a powered airplane.

Almost from the start, the brothers saw that to achieve true flight, they needed to master lift, thrust (power), and control. They noted that little worth-while scientific work had been done in any of these areas. Orville and Wilbur started by studying lift and control with kites. Their first five-foot biplane kite resembled a box kite that Australian Lawrence Hargrave had invented in 1893. Hargrave suggested that such a construction would provide the basis for a stable, practical airplane.

In May 1899, Wilbur Wright wrote to the Smithsonian Institution to request information about heavier-than-air flight. He received several pamphlets about individuals who, although they had for the most part failed in their attempts to fly, were inspirational to the Wrights. The two brothers noted that the most obvious shortcoming in all of these efforts was a lack of concern over controlling a machine once it left the ground.

To test their ideas for controlled flight, the Wrights flew their biplane kite with multiple lines. Pulling some of them moved the upper wing and the horizontal tail. With another pair of lines, they could bend, or "warp," the outer portions of the

> I wish to avail myself of all that is already known [about flying machines] and then if possible add my mite to help the future worker who will attain final success.
> —Wilbur Wright, in his 1899 letter to the Smithsonian Institution

wings in opposite directions. This warping made the kite bank and turn, much like a bird. With this simple kite, the Wright brothers were learning how to control a machine that would fly through the air.

By the late summer of 1900, the two brothers felt they were ready to test a glider that was large enough to carry a human being. They picked a desolate area on the coast of North Carolina because it had the strong, steady winds that were necessary for testing a full-size glider. Their biplane glider had a pair of 17-foot wings that could be warped for steering; a flat elevator, or movable wing, in front that could raise and lower the nose; and an 18-inch space on the lower wing for the pilot to lie on his stomach. The comforts of modern airplanes were lacking, but the necessary controls—however primitive—were there.

For their first Kitty Hawk experiments, the Wright brothers built a glider that could be flown either as a kite or a piloted craft. This allowed them to test the control system without endangering themselves as so many early would-be flyers had done.

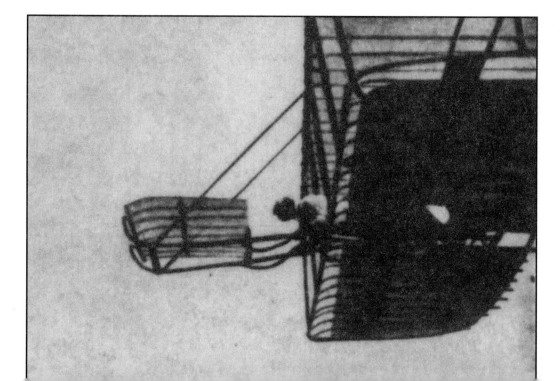

THE BREAKTHROUGH

During most of their experimenting at Kitty Hawk, North Carolina, the Wright brothers flew their first full-size glider as a crewless kite, standing on the ground and moving the controls as they had with their small kite in Dayton. They also flew the "kite" with one of them on board for a few seconds at a time to get the feel of flying. Over the duration of the summer, these short flights totaled less than five minutes.

By the end of their first season at Kitty Hawk, however, the Wrights had made about a dozen flights free of any ground controls. These flights lasted as long as 15 seconds and convinced them that they needed to spend as much time as possible gliding freely down the North Carolina sand dunes and learning to fly. They returned to Dayton in good spirits and with high hopes for the next summer.

In Dayton, they again worked in their bicycle shop, earning the money they would need to pursue their dream of flying. They also began to build their new glider. On July 10, 1901, they were back at Kitty Hawk, ready to resume their gliding experiments. The new glider had two wings with a 22-foot span and an elevator in front to control climbing and diving. New on this second glider was a "hip cradle" that the pilot, lying on his stomach, could use to control the wing-warping system by leaning to the left or to the right.

The brothers were optimistic about this larger machine, but their experiments did not live up to

The actual site of the Wright brothers' camp was at Kill Devil Hills, some four miles from Kitty Hawk.

The steady winds and soft, sandy hills near Kitty Hawk, North Carolina, provided the perfect conditions for the Wright brothers' early experiments.

their expectations. Hoping to remedy problems with lift, they reduced the curvature of the wings, which had been designed according to Otto Lilienthal's measurements. This change improved the lift dramatically and also proved to the Wrights that the data they had originally used was not always fully reliable. Now they were flying with better lift—and also with the knowledge that they would have to rely on their own experiments and calculations.

In 1902, the Wrights built a glider with a 32-foot wingspan (10 feet longer than before), less curve to the wings, a rigid tail, and a larger front elevator.

The new wings provided greater lifting force, and the more elaborate control system was easier to operate. In their tests at Kitty Hawk that summer, the brothers discovered that their new glider was much more efficient than their earlier designs.

Despite these improvements, the Wrights noticed that their glider sometimes banked in the opposite direction from its turn. To correct this flaw, they connected the tail (which had been rigid) to the wing-warping controls so they would operate as one unit. With this change, the task of flying became much easier, and the brothers' piloting skills quickly improved. Soon they could turn in either direction while keeping their glider under control.

By the time Orville and Wilbur left North Carolina that year, they had glided down various sand dunes more than 700 times, taking turns at piloting and guiding the craft from the ground. Their best flight had exceeded 622 feet and lasted 26 seconds. With their increased control and understanding of flight, the brothers were becoming the world's first true pilots.

The Wright brothers had developed a glider that they could fly under full control at almost any time they wished. But their goal was not simply to glide. Instead, they wanted to fly a powered airplane.

Their first "flyer" would have to be an almost completely new design. It could not be simply a glider with an engine added. Instead, it would have to be larger and stronger with longer wings and a shorter fuselage.

fuselage: the body of an aircraft

The biggest obstacle facing the Wrights was finding a light, yet powerful, engine. Unable to locate a manufacturer who would build what they wanted, the brothers had to design their own internal-combustion engine. With their chief mechanic, Charlie Taylor, they produced a motor similar to the kind that powered the automobiles of the day. The four-cylinder engine produced 13 hp—at least until it overheated, which cracked its metal casing.

Once the Wrights and Charlie Taylor had conquered most of the engine's problems, the brothers examined the existing aviation literature to see if there was any useful information about propeller design. Orville wrote to a colleague in June 1903:

> We had been unable to find anything of value in any of the works to which we had access, so that we worked out a theory of our own on the subject, and soon discovered, as we usually do, that all the propellers built heretofore are all wrong, and then built a pair of propellers 8 1/8 ft. in diameter, based on our theory, which were all right! (til we have a chance to test them down at Kitty Hawk and find out differently). Isn't it astonishing that all of these secrets have been preserved for so many years just so that we could discover them!!

Their motor turned their newly designed propellers with a series of sprockets and bicycle chains. The 1903 *Flyer*, as they called their airplane, had a 40-foot wingspan and weighed about 750 pounds, including the pilot. Most of this weight was the heavy motor, propellers, chains, and fuel tank. The wooden frame was constructed from spruce and ash and covered with the finest "Pride of the West" brand of linen.

Orville and Wilbur Wright arrived at Kitty Hawk in late September 1903. Immediately, they set out to rebuild their 1902 camp building, which had been damaged by high winds. Then they constructed a second building that would serve as the hangar for the world's first true airplane.

In order to regain their flying skills, the brothers began by repairing their 1902 glider and starting a new series of glides down the sand dunes. As weeks passed and the various parts for their airplane arrived from Dayton, they began to assemble their new craft. At the same time, they continued to practice gliding.

Although it looked like an astonishingly simple craft, with its engine mounted directly on the lower wing and its propellers turned by bicycle chains, the Wrights' 1903 Flyer *became the first successful powered and controllable airplane in history.*

Soon, they performed two glides of just over a minute and another almost as long, both unofficial world records. Such steady improvements showed they understood what made machines fly.

To launch the glider down the dune, two men needed to run alongside it, each holding a wingtip to keep it steady, until it became airborne. The Wrights knew, however, that their airplane would have to be able to take off from level ground, fly, and then land on ground or sand that was at least as high as the ground from which it had taken off.

To accomplish this feat, the Wrights constructed a specialized launching system. It consisted of a 60-foot single-rail track that supported a small wooden trolley that was mounted on modified bicycle wheels. The wheeled trolley would roll down the track carrying the airplane and would then remain on the ground after the airplane took off. This contraption, which they dubbed the "Grand Junction Railroad," served as a portable runway that the brothers could take virtually anywhere.

The Wright brothers were certain that all future airplanes would use a takeoff device similar to their "Grand Junction Railroad" track.

For landing gear, the brothers designed skids that acted like skis. The Wrights did not build wheels for their plane. Even after other pilots were taking off and landing much more easily with airplanes that had wheels, the Wrights stubbornly stuck to their original construction.

By early November 1903, the Wrights had assembled their airplane and had it ready for testing. But the first time the brothers ran the engine, it vibrated so badly that it damaged one of the propeller shafts. Because of a long series of similar breakdowns and more repairs, it was well into December before the Wrights could attempt to fly under power. In fact, Orville had to return to Dayton to repair some shafts himself to make sure that they would be delivered before it became too cold to fly.

The Wright brothers were in a great hurry to get their airplane into the air because they knew that every delay increased the chance of their rivals, Samuel Langley and Charles Manly, beating them to the first flight. When he was returning from Dayton by train on December 8, Orville learned that Langley's *Aerodrome* had flopped into the Potomac River for a second time. This news meant that Orville and Wilbur could become the first true airplane pilots to conquer the skies.

On the morning of December 12, the brothers installed the new, reinforced shafts on the *Flyer*. Then they rolled their aircraft out of its shed and mounted it on the launching track. But the wind wasn't strong enough for them to fly.

Because the Wrights had promised their clergyman father that they would not fly on Sundays, they had to wait until Monday, December 14, to attempt their flight. The winds that morning were still too calm for taking off from level ground, so they moved their 60-foot launching track to the slope of the largest dune and prepared for a downhill launch.

Wilbur won the coin toss that determined who would make the first attempt. He lay down on the airplane's lower wing with his hips in the padded

Whereas Samuel Langley had chosen to call his airplanes "aerodromes," the Wright brothers called their machines "flyers." Neither name caught on.

wing-warping cradle. Its motor was fired up, and the propellers whirled. Orville ran alongside the plane, balancing one wingtip until the craft could gain flying speed.

When Wilbur pulled the elevator up to make the nose rise, he tugged too hard. The plane reared up and then slipped backward. It hit the ground and swung around, breaking one of the landing skids and several other wooden parts.

Even though it had lifted a man into the air, Wilbur had not really had the craft under control. So they did not consider his flight to be a true one. The brothers, however, had learned that their launching system worked and also that their plane had more than enough power to boost itself into the air. With better handling of the controls, they knew they could fly.

After the two men repaired their plane, they had to wait three more days until the wind picked up again. On Thursday, December 17, 1903, everything finally seemed ready for Orville to make his first attempt at controlled flight. The wind blew at just over 20 mph, so the brothers were able to place the starting rail on a level stretch of ground. Then the Wrights sent out a signal to alert five men who had agreed to help them shift their hulking airplane onto the track. Before long the craft was ready to fly.

Orville lay down on the wing and started the engine, allowing it to warm up, which was difficult on such a cold, bleak day. At half past ten in the morning, one of the helpers released the restraining rope, and the airplane moved forward with Wilbur steadying its right wingtip. By the time the aircraft reached the end of the 60-foot launching track, its speed was 30 mph, and it was already a few feet in the air.

As Orville held the controls steady, the airplane slowly gained altitude and flew across the sands of Kitty Hawk. Up and down the craft went, as its pilot struggled to learn just how much to move the front elevator. Twelve seconds after the plane had left the rail, it bumped into the sand and stopped. A ragged journey of only 120 feet had begun the age of flight.

The Wrights, however, wasted no time in congratulating themselves. Helped by their observers, they hauled the *Flyer* back to its starting point and quickly repaired a cracked skid. The brothers' flights improved as they discovered that their controls responded more quickly during faster powered flights than while gliding more slowly.

The fourth and final flight of the day was the longest. Wilbur stayed in the air for 59 seconds and traveled 852 feet before crashing and badly damaging the airplane's frame. Although their airplane was broken, the two men had accomplished their goal. They had flown!

Before setting off for home, Orville sent a telegram to his father with the news of their success and told him to inform the press. Although the reaction of the press was minimal—for who could believe it?—the two brothers from Dayton were satisfied with their achievement.

Referring to his flight of December 17, 1903, Orville said that it was "the first in the history of the world in which a machine carrying a man had raised itself by its own power into the air in full flight, had sailed forward without reduction of speed, and had finally landed at a point as high as that from which it started."

THE RESULT

The Wright brothers did not return to Kitty Hawk for several years. Instead, they flew at Huffman Prairie outside Dayton, at what is now Wright-Patterson Air Force Base. Their second airplane, the 1904 *Flyer*, flew more than 100 times. In 1905, a third airplane made more than 40 flights and once stayed in the air long enough to travel 24 miles.

By the end of 1905, the brothers had made more than 150 flights and had accumulated many hours of flying experience. As yet, no one else had made a recognized flight. While someone possibly may have made a controlled flight before the Wright brothers, only the flights of Orville and Wilbur Wright led to progress in flying.

Gustave Whitehead (shown here with his daughter) is one of many who said he had made a controlled flight before the Wright brothers. He claimed that he had flown his craft for seven miles over New York's Long Island Sound in 1902.

Since 1903, engineers, designers, and factory personnel have built well over 1 million airplanes in huge factories and home workshops, and billions of people have flown for business and pleasure. All these planes and flights owe a debt to a pair of quiet, studious brothers who applied the logic of science to flight and left the ground one day in December of 1903. The 1903 Wright *Flyer* is now on display in the National Air and Space Museum in Washington, D.C., along with two other historic Wright airplanes: the first military plane and the first airplane to fly across the United States.

As Orville left the launching track on the morning of December 17, 1903, John Daniels, one of the local men who had helped lift the Flyer into position, snapped one of the greatest news photographs ever: the first controlled flight.

CHAPTER SIX

Glenn Curtiss and the Seaplane

It was a craving for speed that brought the next great innovator to the field of aviation. Born on May 21, 1878, in Hammondsport, New York, Glenn Hammond Curtiss was an inventive youth who could build almost anything from whatever bits and pieces were lying around. When he became dissatisfied with the speed he could achieve while ice skating on Lake Keuka near his home, Curtiss constructed a sail to harness the power of the wind. As an adult, Curtiss would soar over Lake Keuka in seaplanes he had designed.

Although Glenn Curtiss was a hard-working, serious young man, he was only an average student. After one year of high school, he dropped out to help support his family. Before taking a job as a telegraph messenger, Glenn worked for Eastman Kodak, the world's leading manufacturer of cameras and photographic film. At Kodak, he earned enough money to buy his first bicycle.

Before taking an interest in aviation, Glenn Hammond Curtiss (1878-1930) built and raced bicycles and motorcycles. For his innovations in the field of seaplanes, Curtiss has been called the "Father of Naval Aviation."

89

By the time he was 19, Curtiss had opened a small bicycle shop. His love of speed led him to race his bicycles, just as Orville Wright had done. In 1901, Curtiss established his own bicycle-manufacturing company in his hometown of Hammondsport. It did not take long for him to explore the possibility of powering his bicycles with a motor. Curtiss began to tinker with gasoline-powered engines and soon produced one that could move his motorized cycle at 30 mph, an amazing speed at that time. Before long, the G. H. Curtiss Manufacturing Company was selling motorcycles to eager customers all over the country.

Consumed by his quest for speed, Curtiss built and raced some of the fastest machines of his day. He thought that racing in public exhibitions would be good advertising for his business—and he was right. The Curtiss name soon became synonymous with high-quality, lightweight engines and fast motorcycles. In 1904, this reputation led an aviation innovator named Thomas Baldwin to order a Curtiss engine to power a new airship he had designed.

Thomas Baldwin, a former circus performer, had seen a Curtiss motorcycle in California and was so impressed by its motor that he decided to use one for his airship, the *California Arrow*. Built to carry two people, the *California Arrow* began making remarkable flights and attracting the attention of people interested in flying. Although Glenn Curtiss was not involved in building the airship, Baldwin moved his balloon-manufacturing facilities from California to Hammondsport and began working

Aeronaut Thomas Baldwin saw a motorcycle on a ranch near San Francisco. Admiring the engine, he inquired about its make. Glenn Curtiss's career in aviation began when the driver told Baldwin it was a Curtiss.

with Curtiss. The two men eventually provided the U.S. Army with its first dirigible, the *Signal Corps Dirigible Number 1.*

During this time, however, Curtiss was more interested in motors and motorcycles than in flying. In January 1907, he traveled to Florida to race and attempt to set a speed record. For this event, he built a huge motorcycle equipped with a V-8 engine. Driving this super-powered machine at 137 mph, Curtiss roared along a one-mile course in just 26 seconds, setting a world's record that would stand until 1911, when an automobile reached a speed of 141 mph. But for now, Glenn Curtiss was the fastest man in the world.

On his way to Florida, Curtiss met Alexander Graham Bell, who had invented the telephone in 1876. At the time, Bell was busy trying to develop a kite that could carry people, and he asked Curtiss to build an engine that would provide thrust for his contraption. Their meeting would lead to the formation of the Aerial Experiment Association (AEA) on October 1, 1907, and to Glenn Curtiss's involvement in the young field of aviation. Curtiss was named director of experiments for the AEA, and he traveled to Baddeck, Nova Scotia, where Bell had been experimenting with large kites.

Once the AEA began working on a powered airplane, progress was rapid. With army lieutenant Thomas Selfridge acting as lead designer, *Drome Number 1* (nicknamed the *Red Wing* for its red silk covering) was ready to fly in seven weeks. The craft's first and last flight was on March 12, 1908, when

When asked about his world-record run on the sands of Ormond Beach in Florida, Glenn Curtiss replied, "It satisfied my craving for speed."

As a friend of Samuel Langley, Alexander Graham Bell was pleased that his AEA team used Langley's term "aerodrome" to refer to their early experimental crafts.

Members of the Aerial Experiment Association in 1908. Shown (left to right) are Frederick "Casey" Baldwin, Thomas Selfridge, Glenn Curtiss, Alexander Graham Bell, and Jack McCurdy. Augustus Post, president of the Aero Club of America, stands at the far right.

---

ailerons: movable flaps on the wings of airplanes used to control rolling and banking

---

Frederick "Casey" Baldwin (no relation to Thomas Baldwin) took off and climbed eight feet. He flew almost 319 feet before crashing. Although the plane had been damaged beyond repair, the Curtiss engine could be used again, and Baldwin escaped injury. The team, therefore, considered this first flight a success.

On May 22, 1908, Curtiss flew the *White Wing*, the AEA's second "aerodrome," more than 1,000 feet on his first attempt. This second machine had been equipped with ailerons, or wing flaps, which provided the lateral (banking) control that had been lacking in the *Red Wing*. It also had a three-wheeled undercarriage for landing, which was a logical advance that the Wrights would resist for some years. Glenn Curtiss had now experienced controlled flight with its promise of speed. This adventure inspired him to press on with new ideas and innovations.

From then on, the advances came quickly. Curtiss supervised the building of the next AEA aerodrome, the *June Bug*, with improved ailerons and landing gear. He would fly the *June Bug* in an attempt to win the *Scientific American* magazine's trophy—worth $2500—for being the first person to fly one kilometer (0.62 mile) in a straight line. The magazine wanted to encourage American inventors "by giving them a valuable object of art worth winning." In offering the trophy, the magazine was also attempting to coax Orville and Wilbur Wright into making public their flight experiments.

The Wrights did not attempt to win the prize, so Curtiss saw this as an opportunity to add an aviation trophy to his already impressive collection of awards and also to improve the reputation of the AEA. On July 4, 1908, at Stony Brook Farm near Hammondsport, Glenn Curtiss flew farther than the required one kilometer and won the *Scientific American* Trophy.

Even though Wilbur Wright had flown farther than Glenn Curtiss, his flights had not been widely reported, so few people knew about them—and even fewer believed they had happened. Curtiss's flight, however, had been made before hundreds of reporters, scientists, and curious onlookers. He had proven to a skeptical American public that an airplane could fly with a human on board.

Flying over Stony Brook Farm in the June Bug *on the Fourth of July, Glenn Curtiss made the first successful flight in the United States that was viewed by the public.*

Next, Curtiss turned his attention to building a seaplane. His plan was to attach pontoons to his successful *June Bug* and then take off from water. After he replaced the wheels of the *June Bug* with large, canoe-like pontoons, he gave his modified craft a more water-friendly name: the *Loon*. Curtiss made several attempts to fly the *Loon* on Lake Keuka but found that it had too little power. Although it could skim across the lake at 25 mph, the *Loon* could not lift itself out of the water and fly.

Earlier, the Wright brothers had conducted similar unsuccessful pontoon experiments. But Curtiss persisted because he was convinced there was a greater need for fast transportation across water than over land. While trains were becoming increasingly common and operated at high speeds, the fastest passenger ships were far slower. Seaplanes would drastically cut the time it took to cross the Atlantic Ocean, with the rivers, lakes, and oceans of the world providing instant, inexpensive runways.

Leaving a cloud of dust and exhaust in his wake, Curtiss raced the June Bug *before hundreds of witnesses.*

The scheme of starting a flying machine from and landing on water has been in my mind for some time. It has many advantages, and I believe it can be worked out.

—Glenn Curtiss

Among the favored competitors at the Rheims air meet was Louis Blériot of France, who on July 25, 1909, had become the first human to cross the English Channel in an airplane. (He is shown here with his wife shortly after the historic flight.)

THE BREAKTHROUGH

Recognizing the potential of the seaplane, Glenn Curtiss planned to build a practical machine that would earn large profits for his company. But before he could begin to design the plane, the Aero Club of America asked him to represent the United States in an international air meet in France. Before Curtiss left for France, he won the second leg of the *Scientific American* Trophy on July 17, 1909. In that contest, he flew the *Gold Bug*, the first aircraft he had built independent of the AEA, in a circle for 25 miles. Curtiss then ended his association with the AEA and began working on another airplane for the August meet in Rheims, France.

Curtiss arrived in Rheims with his new plane, the *Golden Flyer* (sometimes called the *Rheims Racer*).

It was similar to the earlier *Gold Bug*, except for its much larger 50 hp V-8 engine and propeller. To the surprise of the Europeans—and the elation of the Americans in attendance—Curtiss beat the world's best flyers to win the Gordon Bennett Cup. Curtiss was now internationally famous, and orders poured in for his airplanes and engines.

In February 1909, the *New York World* newspaper had offered a $10,000 prize to the first person who flew along the Hudson River between New York City and Albany (allowing stops for refueling and to make repairs), a distance of 150 miles. No one tried in 1909, but by 1910, Curtiss was hard at work on a new airplane that was built specifically for that flight. He would call this plane the *Hudson Flyer*. Because there might not be a landing field in sight when he needed it, Curtiss installed pontoons on the plane so he could land on the river if that became necessary. The seaplane was born with a test landing on Lake Keuka on May 22, 1910. Because the *Hudson Flyer* also had wheels for taking off from and landing on the ground, Curtiss called the craft an amphibian.

On May 23, Curtiss formally announced that he would try for the *New York World* prize three days later. Technical delays and bad weather, however, prevented him from flying until Sunday, May 29. Early that morning, Curtiss took off, heading down the Hudson River from Albany and racing a train that had been chartered by the *New York Times* to carry observers and reporters. Both shores of the river were lined with thousands of spectators. Few of

Although the Wright brothers in the United States built and flew the world's first practical airplane in 1903, interest in human flight had been far greater in Europe—especially France—since the Montgolfier brothers first launched their balloon in 1783.

amphibian: an aircraft that can take off from and land on either land or water

On March 28, 1910, Frenchman Henri Fabre had taken off from and landed on the water in his Hydravion. *It was not a practical machine, however, and Fabre never rebuilt his craft after it crashed two months later.*

them had ever seen an airplane—and even fewer were aware that they were witnessing the first demonstration of the seaplane.

Curtiss flew over the bridge at Poughkeepsie, New York, and then landed in a field to refuel. The man who was supposed to be there with the supplies didn't show up, however, because he, like the Wright brothers, observed the Sabbath and did not work on Sundays. Motorists who had come to witness the event volunteered gasoline and oil from their cars, and soon Curtiss continued on. Arriving at New York City, he circled the Statue of Liberty before landing on nearby Governor's Island, where he was hailed by enormous crowds. For his 2-hour, 46-minute flight, Curtiss was celebrated as a brave pilot and a pioneering designer and builder.

Curtiss basked in the fame that his triumph had brought him. For a time, he traveled the country making exhibition flights. Everyone wanted to see Glenn Hammond Curtiss fly, and they were willing to pay for it. But soon Curtiss decided to focus his attention on producing and selling airplanes. Because the benefits of air travel were becoming more widely accepted, Curtiss realized that the United States military would be looking for airplanes, and he would be ready to supply them.

The U.S. Army had already begun working with the Wright brothers, so Curtiss set his sights on developing seaplanes for the U.S. Navy. The navy's first requirement was that the planes be able to take off from and land on a ship's deck. The Wright brothers had declined this challenge, believing it was

too dangerous. But Curtiss jumped at the opportunity because he recognized this as his chance to secure business with the navy.

On November 14, 1910, Eugene Ely took off in Curtiss's modified *Golden Flyer* from a special platform on the deck of the navy's USS *Birmingham*. The following January, Ely both landed on and took off from a similar platform on the USS *Pennsylvania*.

While Ely's feat was impressive, it was not enough to convince the navy to invest in a fleet of Curtiss aircraft. They thought that having airplanes taking off from and landing on the decks of ships would be dangerous and interfere with ship operations. George von Lengerke Meyer, secretary of the U.S. Navy, told Curtiss that if he could build a plane

Glenn Curtiss pilots one of his first successful seaplanes, or Hydroaeroplanes, as his team referred to the machines.

For his navy demonstrations, Curtiss developed an "arresting gear" to stop the plane when it landed on the deck of the ship. This gear is now standard on all aircraft carriers.

capable of landing in the water next to a ship, being hauled on board with a crane, and then lowered again to the water for takeoff, "I shall be ready to say that the Navy Department is convinced."

Curtiss now leased an island near San Diego, California, to escape the cold New York winters. There, the Curtiss team immediately went to work to produce their first true seaplane. The plane had a more complete boatlike hull and tubular floats on its lower wingtips that would prevent it from capsizing. On February 17, 1911, Curtiss was ready to land alongside the USS *Pennsylvania*. By making good on Secretary Meyer's challenge, Glenn Curtiss and his seaplane gave birth to naval aviation.

Curtiss and his seaplane are hoisted aboard the USS Pennsylvania *on February 17, 1911—a day that marked the beginning of a strong working relationship between the U.S. Navy and Glenn Curtiss.*

THE RESULT

Curtiss quickly supplied the navy with its first aircraft, the *Triad*, which could operate on land, on water, and in the air. Orders for seaplanes followed shortly, both from the imperial navies of Europe and from wealthy sportsmen who wanted to experience this versatile flying machine. Always a shrewd businessman, Curtiss offered free lessons to potential navy pilots and even invited the navy to share his island near San Diego. They accepted both offers. This strengthened Curtiss's relationship with the navy and secured his prominent role in the navy's growing air program.

Glenn Curtiss (center) with his first class of U.S. Navy pilots. The Curtiss School of Aviation began operating in December 1910 and instructed both military and civilian students in the art of flying.

Glenn Curtiss worked with the U.S. Navy to develop the NC-4 flying boat, the first aircraft to cross the Atlantic Ocean. The "NC" stood for "Navy Curtiss" and indicated the teamwork that had gone into building the craft.

One early Curtiss seaplane, the *America*, was put into naval service as an antisubmarine patrol craft in World War I. Its design became the standard seaplane for the British, and the war years proved to be very profitable for Glenn Curtiss.

The *America* actually had been built to fly across the Atlantic Ocean. In 1913, the *Daily Mail* newspaper of London had offered a prize of £10,000 (about $50,000 in today's money) for the first non-stop transatlantic flight. But World War I began in Europe in 1914, so Curtiss put his plans on hold.

The first flight across the Atlantic (with stops to refuel) would be made some years later by a much larger Curtiss seaplane, the *NC-4*, which had four 400 hp engines and a 126-foot wingspan. Navy commander Albert Read and his crew flew the *NC-4* into the harbor at Lisbon, Portugal, on May 27, 1919, after leaving Newfoundland in Canada 11 days earlier. With the help of the U.S. Navy, Curtiss and his team had conquered the Atlantic.

Seaplanes soon grew larger and faster and capable of flying longer distances without stopping. During World War II, they carried enormous loads of cargo, protected convoys of freighters from submarine attack, and also rescued downed pilots. But as more long concrete runways were built for land-based airplanes, seaplanes began to fade away. Because they needed boat-shaped hulls to operate on the water, they were not as streamlined as airplanes flying from the land, and they could not cruise as fast or as economically. Seaplanes also had limited ability to land in ice-filled waters.

Today, flying boats are used mainly to carry water to fight forest fires. A firefighting flying boat can take on thousands of gallons of water by skimming over a lake and then flying over the forest fire, dropping its cargo on the flames. And small float-planes are used to transport sportsmen to hunting and fishing areas that lack airports for landing. The great era of the seaplane is gone. Thanks to the brilliance of men like Glenn Curtiss, however, seaplanes filled a critical niche in early aviation.

Both the *NC-4* and the *America* were **flying boats**, seaplanes on which the hull-shaped fuselage acts as the main flotation surface for operation from water. This characteristic distinguished these planes from **float planes**, seaplanes that are mounted on pontoons for operation from water.

CHAPTER SEVEN

Igor Sikorsky and the Helicopter

For the first few hundred years of dreaming and scheming about flight, visionaries gave little thought to aircraft that needed long takeoff runs to get into the air. Because the way to the sky was obviously straight up, they believed pilots could achieve that feat either by imitating birds or building rotary-winged helicopters.

As early as 1460, street vendors sold wind-up helicopter toys on the streets of Paris. These toys consisted of a stick with a simple propeller (called an airscrew) at each end. Twisted elastic turned the two propellers in opposite directions. When a child wound the elastic tightly and let go, the toy lurched upward for a few feet of flight. Innovators interested in flight thought they could build a helicopter capable of carrying people simply by building a much larger toy. With larger propellers—later called rotors—and some sort of engine to turn them, a pilot should be able to fly straight up.

After establishing himself as a top airplane designer in his Russian homeland, Igor Ivanovich Sikorsky (1889-1972) emigrated to the United States, where he once again rose to the top of the aviation field.

Leonardo da Vinci's sketch of a helicopter is said to have been Sikorsky's original inspiration for building his own helicopter.

Getting a helicopter to fly, however, proved to be far more complicated than anyone could have imagined. Like the people who were trying to design airplanes, the designers of helicopters also faced problems of stability, control, and the need for a powerful but lightweight engine. Sometime around 1490, Leonardo da Vinci, the ingenious Italian artist, inventor, and scientist, had sketched a model for a powered helicopter. Yet centuries would pass before an engine-driven helicopter would fly.

In 1842, Englishman W. H. Phillips flew a steam-powered model to what then seemed a "great altitude," but which was probably no more than a few feet in the air. Still, his invention was important because everyone else had tried only to improve on the fifteenth-century elastic-driven toys.

In the years that followed Phillips's experiment, wild schemes appeared alongside more carefully thought-out designs. In 1863, Frenchman Gabriel de la Landelle proposed an unworkable invention consisting of a ship's hull, two stacks of four rotor blades (each equipped with a parachute), two wings, and a steam engine. That same year, Frenchman viscomte de Ponton d'Amécourt built a small helicopter with a compact little steam engine that drove two rotors. His craft almost lifted off the ground.

In 1905, Maurice Leger in Monaco experimented with a full-scale helicopter that had two 20-foot rotors, turned by an electric motor attached to batteries on the ground. Although the machine lifted slightly, it did not truly fly because the length of its power cord limited how high it could go.

Like all novices, we began with the helicopter but soon saw that it had no future and dropped it.
—Wilbur Wright

These early inventors had attempted to prove that full-size helicopters could fly. Now they turned to designing and building a helicopter that could carry at least one person aloft.

In Douai, France, on September 29, 1907, less than four years after the Wright brothers flew their first airplane, a man named Volumard became the first person to lift off in a helicopter. The helicopter, designed by Louis Breguet (who would later gain fame as an airplane manufacturer), did not achieve a truly free flight because several men had to brace the machine to keep it from tipping over as it hovered. But Breguet's invention had lifted a human about a foot off the ground for almost a minute.

Less than two months later, near Lisieux, France, Paul Cornu flew without any assistance from people on the ground and stayed up for more than 20 seconds. With only two three-bladed rotors, his helicopter needed just 24 hp to get off the ground. It lacked, however, the built-in stability and effective controls to keep it level.

Now the man who would become the first major figure in the history of helicopters appeared on the scene. Igor Ivanovich Sikorsky was born to a well-to-do family in Kiev, Russia, on May 25, 1889. Sikorsky's father, a renowned psychiatrist, was as dedicated to science as he was to his family. But it was Igor's mother, a medical school graduate, who filled Sikorsky's head with dreams of vertical flight by telling him about Leonardo's ideas for helicopters.

At age 14, Sikorsky entered the Imperial Russian Naval Academy in St. Petersburg and served

With an eight-cylinder engine tucked between his legs, Paul Cornu made the first free flight in a helicopter on November 13, 1907.

As a teenager, Igor Sikorsky found an anarchist pamphlet that included plans for making a bomb. Soon he was entertaining workmen from the neighborhood with explosions in his family's garden.

In 1908, Wilbur Wright sailed to Europe to show the Wright *Flyer* to prospective buyers, such as the French government. Wilbur's test flights and exhibitions in France and Germany were extremely successful that year; he sold lucrative contracts to French manufacturers to produce Wright airplanes and was also hailed by the European public.

as a naval cadet for three years. Feeling he was not suited for the military, Sikorsky left the academy in 1906 and studied engineering briefly in Paris before returning home to study electrical engineering at the Polytechnic Institute of Kiev. Sikorsky was a good student, but he found the work that he did in his workshop at home more interesting than his academic pursuits. While visiting Germany with his father in 1908, Sikorsky read about and saw photographs of Wilbur Wright's European flights. Realizing that human flight was actually possible, Sikorsky decided to pursue aviation seriously.

Sikorsky's goal was to build a helicopter. A successful helicopter would need a strong and lightweight power supply. Lightweight gasoline engines were being developed at that time but were not available in Russia. So, with money borrowed from his sister, Olga, Sikorsky returned to Paris in 1909 to purchase a suitable motor to power his first helicopter. He settled on a 25 hp, three-cylinder Anzani engine, the same type that Louis Blériot would use in his flight across the English Channel later that year.

While in France—still the center of the world of aviation—Sikorsky learned all that he could about flight. He even took some classes from renowned French aviator Captain Ferdinand Ferber. When Sikorsky told Ferber about his plans to build a helicopter, Ferber told him to focus on airplanes. "You will waste your time on a helicopter," he declared.

Undeterred, Sikorsky returned to Kiev and, within two months, he had built his first helicopter. The machine had a wooden frame that supported his new engine and provided a place for a pilot to sit. Two hollow shafts ran up from the engine, and there were two double-bladed rotors at the top of each shaft. These simple rotors were turned in opposite directions by wooden pulleys and flexible belts.

From July until October, Sikorsky tested his machine and modified and tested it again, all without any hint of success. Although the engine and rotors developed around 350 pounds of thrust, the entire machine weighed 450 pounds, so it was too heavy to lift itself off the ground. The young visionary gave up on his first helicopter and returned to Paris.

In Paris, Sikorsky bought two more engines and tried to learn more about aviation. When he returned to Russia, he began experimenting with propeller-driven sleighs that he drove through Kiev's snowy streets. In February 1910, he took the engine from his sleigh and installed it on his new helicopter. Although this helicopter was lighter and had improved rotors, it, too, failed to get off the ground.

While working on his second helicopter, Sikorsky also began work on an airplane, perhaps feeling this would provide a quicker route to the skies. Within a few months, he had designed and built three planes and had flown two of them. Although both soon crashed, they taught him enough about designing to give him confidence in his ability to create flying machines.

By the spring of 1911, the 21-year-old Sikorsky had built his first durable airplane, the *S-5*. He learned to fly with this plane and was issued the 64th pilot's license granted by the Russian authorities.

Sikorsky poses with his second helicopter at the family's home in Kiev in 1910. Although it produced substantial lift, the machine's 400-pound weight was more than its 25 hp engine could handle.

The following winter, Sikorsky built the *S-6*. This was his first craft that was not based on earlier French designs. The *S-6* could carry three passengers at 70 mph—an impressive speed in those days.

In February 1912, an improved *S-6* won first prize in an international competition sponsored by the Imperial Russian Army. Unlike the total frustration of trying to invent the helicopter, Sikorsky's airplane efforts were paying off rapidly, and his reputation as a top designer grew as his achievements became better known. A few months later, Sikorsky was offered and accepted a job as designer and chief engineer of the newly formed aviation branch of a large manufacturing firm in St. Petersburg.

Now, with a real factory and paid workers, the young Russian began to investigate the idea of building a larger airplane. Sikorsky built his machine over the winter of 1912, and it was ready to fly on May 13, 1913. With four 100 hp engines and a wingspan of 92 feet, the *Grand* dwarfed anything previously built. Many feared that such a large machine would not fly. But those people were wrong, and the *Grand* was an astounding success. Two months later, Sikorsky received an invitation to demonstrate the *Grand* for Tsar Nicholas II of Russia. No longer a teenager tinkering with helicopters in his backyard, Sikorsky was a successful designer and aviator.

A second four-engine craft, the *Ilia Mourometz* (named for a Russian folk hero), followed. With the outbreak of World War I in 1914, the *Ilia Mourometz* became Russia's standard large bomber, and 73 were put into service for the military. But even before the war ended, the Russian Revolution had begun in 1917, bringing Vladimir Lenin and the Bolsheviks to power. With his ties to the former regime of Tsar Nicholas II, Sikorsky feared that he, like many of his military associates, would be arrested and executed as an "enemy of the people." So Igor Sikorsky fled to the West, first to London and later to Paris.

When World War I ended in 1918, Sikorsky considered staying in France, but he felt that his opportunities would be greater in the United States. After arriving in New York in March 1919, Sikorsky immediately set out to take advantage of his worldwide reputation by designing a new bomber for the

In 1913, Tsar Nicholas II made an official inspection of Sikorsky's Grand, *the world's first four-engine aircraft. Impressed by the craft and its young designer, Nicholas sent Sikorsky a gold watch bearing the imperial Russian eagle.*

Vladimir Lenin and the Bolsheviks took power in Russia in 1917 and later murdered Nicholas II and his family.

A gift of $5,000 from the Russian composer Sergei Rachmaninoff helped keep Sikorsky's fledgling company operating during its early years.

U.S. Army. But while his ideas impressed the military, Congress did not give the peacetime army enough money to fund Sikorsky's airplane.

In 1923, Sikorsky organized the Sikorsky Aero Engineering Corporation and began working on his *S-29-A*. The financially struggling company built the frame for this plane with metal from bedsprings that had been thrown out by a nearby hospital. Although the *S-29-A* provided good publicity for the company, it did not attract orders for more airplanes. So it was back to the drawing board for Sikorsky and his team.

A string of one-of-a-kind airplanes followed until 1926, when Sikorsky's interests shifted to seaplanes and amphibians—planes that could operate from water or land. Like Glenn Curtiss, he realized that most large cities were located near bodies of water that could provide "runways" for large watercraft. By including retractable wheels, Sikorsky's amphibians could take off from land as well as water.

Between 1926 and 1942, Sikorsky built more than 200 amphibians and seaplanes that were purchased by major airlines as well as the U.S. Navy. The final Sikorsky seaplane—the VS-44—operated on the Atlantic Ocean during World War II.

The age of the seaplane came to an end in the early 1940s. During the war, the Allies had built so many large airports with long runways that airlines no longer needed the bulky amphibians that operated mainly from the water. Rather than spend his time bemoaning the loss, Igor Sikorsky now resurrected his earlier dream of developing the helicopter.

THE BREAKTHROUGH

Certain developments had been made since Sikorsky's unsuccessful efforts to construct a workable helicopter before World War I. Propeller (rotor) design had advanced greatly, and engines could now produce horsepower that would have been unimaginable in 1910 when Sikorsky had been tinkering with his 25 hp Anzani engines.

Engineers had built and tested many types of helicopters, and some of them had even worked. A U.S. military engineer named George de Bothezat had constructed a huge, complicated machine for the U.S. Army in the early 1920s. Although the helicopter did work, the army scrapped the project, believing the results did not justify the large investment that was required to continue to improve the machine.

Inventors in France, Spain, Italy, the Netherlands, and Denmark also built and tested other rotary-winged craft. While some of them flew, all of them suffered from a lack of stability and frequent malfunctions of their many complicated parts. The result was far more helicopter crashes than successful flights.

Then, in 1931, aviation pioneer Louis Breguet built the first helicopter that really flew. In 1935, his huge, 350 hp *Breguet-Dorand 314* took off. It flew vertically, made a full circle while rising to 500 feet, and then landed in one piece. On subsequent flights, Breguet stayed up for 45 minutes and flew at speeds as fast as 50 mph.

In 1938, Hanna Reitsch made the first public demonstration flight of the Fa-61 helicopter in Berlin. On June 20 of that year, German test pilot Karl Bode flew the Fa-61 a record distance of 143 miles.

Unlike Sikorsky's later single-rotor helicopters, Heinrich Focke's Fa-61 had two rotors mounted on frames called outriggers that extended from the sides of the fuselage.

In the 1930s, German aviation engineer Heinrich Focke began to develop a helicopter for the Nazis. Although they had denounced Focke because he did not support their regime, the Nazis were forced to rely on his expertise. Focke contributed to the field of vertical flight with his Fa-61, a helicopter with two rotors mounted on outriggers.

Next came Igor Sikorsky. Like the Wright brothers, he first studied and experimented and then slowly improved his working models. In 1938, Sikorsky built a test-bed—a rig consisting of an engine and a rotor that was fixed to the ground. With this contraption, he measured and learned how to control the many forces acting on rotors. His

biggest advance was using a small tail-rotor to counteract torque, the tendency of a helicopter's fuselage to turn in the opposite direction as its rotor.

Having solved a major problem, Sikorsky now set out to build his first helicopter in almost 30 years. With a single, three-bladed main rotor and a small tail-rotor, the VS-300 would be much different and simpler than all known helicopters to date. The main rotor's design owed much to the work of Juan de la Cierva, who created the first autogiro in 1923, and Harold Pitcairn, who also worked with autogiros. Their machines with unpowered rotors had solved some of the problems of rotor construction.

On September 14, 1939—just two weeks after Germany invaded Poland, starting World War II in Europe—Sikorsky first flew the VS-300 helicopter while it was attached by lines to the ground. With the world's attention focused on the war, few people were aware of his historic flight. The initial tethered flight lasted only a few seconds. But, by the end of the day, the 75 hp VS-300 had made several more brief hops and had demonstrated a degree of control and stability that suggested Sikorsky's team (which included several of his Russian émigré friends) was on the right track.

Sikorsky made more flights and continued to modify the craft. Among the important lessons that he learned during this period was how complicated it was to fly a helicopter. Because the craft could do so much more than an airplane—it could fly sideways, backwards, and straight up, and could also hover in one place—it needed many complicated controls.

torque: a turning or twisting force; in an aircraft, torque is caused by the spinning of the propeller or rotor

autogiro: the first rotary-winged aircraft to achieve sustained, controlled flight; like an airplane, it is driven forward by a propeller, and it derives lift from an unpowered rotor (similar to a helicopter's powered rotor) mounted above the fuselage. Unlike the helicopter, the autogiro cannot hover or take off without a runway.

Ever the cautious aviator, Igor Sikorsky made the historic first flight of the VS-300 while tethered to the ground.

On May 6, 1941, Sikorsky flew his VS-300 for 1 hour, 32 minutes, and 26 seconds, breaking the previous world record of 1 hour and 20 minutes that the Fa-61 had held since 1937.

Slowly, the team perfected the controls and learned how to fly the machine.

Although the nation was not yet involved in World War II, the U.S. Army Air Corps was showing an interest in Sikorsky's helicopter. On July 24, 1940, Captain Frank Gregory of the U.S. Army flew the helicopter while visiting the Sikorsky plant in Connecticut. Gregory's two short flights convinced him that the army needed helicopters. Several months later, the Army Air Corps gave Sikorsky a contract to build a two-seat helicopter, which would be called the XR-4 (or the Experimental Rotary-Wing Type 4). With the U.S. Army supporting his helicopter endeavors, Sikorsky would launch this new branch of aviation.

THE RESULT

In January 1942, just weeks after the nation entered World War II, the U.S. Army flew the XR-4, now renamed the R-4, for the first time. Four months later, a pilot flew the craft from the Sikorsky Aero Engineering Corporation in Connecticut to Wright Field in Ohio—a distance of more than 750 miles—in five days.

The R-4 became the first helicopter to go into production after its formal acceptance by the army in May 1942. By the time the war ended in 1945, the Sikorsky company had built 131 of the R-4s, along with hundreds of the more advanced R-5s and R-6s.

When the XR-4 was accepted by the Army and put into production, it was no longer "experimental," and so the "X" was dropped from the name, leaving it the R-4.

Standing in front of Sikorsky's XR-4 are Igor Sikorsky (left) and Orville Wright, two of the greatest innovators the field of aviation has ever known.

By the 1950s, other companies besides Sikorsky's, including Bell, Hughes, and Hiller, had developed and were producing their own helicopters.

The biggest single improvement in helicopters was replacing the piston engine with the gas turbine engine, which could produce much more power. Sikorsky's first turbine helicopter, the XH-39, was ready for flight in 1954 and promptly set world records for speed (156 mph) and altitude (24,521 feet).

The helicopter saw limited action in World War II. Pilots flew them on missions to gather military information and to rescue soldiers, but not in combat. The ability to land and take off in a space no larger than a tennis court gave the helicopter an advantage over the airplane in reaching isolated locations and troops.

The helicopter's potential was more fully realized during the Korean War (1950–1953). By then, it was larger, and the newer machines could handle a wide variety of functions, including evacuating wounded soldiers. When armed with machine guns and rockets, helicopters could also engage in warfare.

Following the Korean War, Sikorsky wasted no time in exploring still more uses for his machine. His S-55, developed originally for the military, led to the first true short-distance passenger helicopter, the S-61, which was used in the United States by the Los Angeles Helicopter Airways and Pan American World Airways. In Europe, Belgium's SABENA airline and British European Airways also flew Sikorsky helicopters on short passenger flights.

In 1962, Sikorsky produced the first helicopter for heavy lifting, the S-64 "Skycrane." It consisted of a standard cockpit, a slender fuselage, and a conventional tail-and-rotor assembly. The main difference between the S-64 and Sikorsky's earlier helicopters was the lack of cargo or passenger space, which was used instead for lifting gear. With this gear, pilots could lift large objects, such as housing modules, building materials, and trucks, and then carry and deposit them in hard-to-reach places.

When Igor Sikorsky died in 1972, he left a legacy of having created the first successful large, multi-engined airplane; some of the finest seaplanes; and, most importantly, the helicopter. His VS-300 was the first single-rotor helicopter to fly under full control while lifting a significant payload, and his R-4 was the first to go into production and then be ready for distribution. But most important, Igor Sikorsky demonstrated that the helicopter was a practical flying machine. Some of his earliest machines are on display in the U.S. Air Force Museum in Dayton, Ohio, and at the Smithsonian Institution in Washington, D.C.

payload: the total weight of passengers and cargo that an aircraft can carry.

Igor Sikorsky had envisioned the helicopter as a machine that anyone could own and use for personal transportation. But, like the R-4 (below), the first helicopter to go into service for the U.S. Army, it has remained predominately a craft for military use.

Faster and Farther

During World War II, the flying machine came of age. A million of them were built between 1939 and 1945—two-thirds of the total number of aircraft produced since the 1903 Wright *Flyer*.

Aircraft had an enormous impact on the war, and the war had just as great an impact on aircraft. In previous wars, most casualties were suffered on or near battlefields, where soldiers fired cannon, rifles, and machine guns. In World War II, however, airplanes flew hundreds of miles to drop millions of pounds of bombs on locations far from the fighting zones, making the home front often as dangerous as the battlefields.

Airplane design experienced amazingly rapid changes during the war. When the war began, many of the world's air forces were equipped with biplanes, airplanes with two wings supported by struts and wires. Pilots sat out in the open, and the wheels of the plane hung below them. Few of the planes could

In 1939, Pan American World Airways purchased 12 Boeing Clipper flying boats for luxurious overseas flights. However, by 1943, Pan American had retired all of the Clippers from service. By then, more airports had been built, and landplanes, such as the Douglas DC-4, which could carry more people and travel faster, had been developed.

The most famous Curtiss aircraft was not a seaplane, but the JN, or "Jenny," which was used by the United States as its primary training craft for pilots during World War I. After the war, surplus Jennys were sold at bargain prices, and daredevil pilots called "barnstormers" purchased the inexpensive machines and then toured the country making exhibition flights.

fly faster than 200 mph or farther than a few hundred miles. By the time the war ended in 1945, sleek monoplanes, whose parts were tucked inside for streamlining, had replaced biplanes. Pilots controlled the plane inside fully enclosed cockpits, and wheels pulled up into wings or fuselages. Speeds had climbed into the 400 mph range and higher.

The most striking change, however, was in the design of the engine. Before the war, only piston engines that turned propellers drove airplanes. While engineers were making such engines larger and more powerful, another change was taking place: the turbojet engine was born. A basically simple device, the turbojet engine operates when air pours into its front and is then heated, mixed with fuel, and ignited. A fierce blast of exhaust shoots out the rear of the engine and pushes the plane forward. The first jet engines did not produce much power and wore out quickly, but they soon boasted several times the power of piston engines of similar size.

Jet-powered airplanes, however, had surprisingly little impact on the outcome of World War II. The Nazis used several types of these planes in combat, but they were not well developed. In fact, the Allies shot down more German jets in their propeller-driven planes than they lost to the enemy jets.

After the war, the future clearly lay with jet airplanes. Before long, factory workers were producing the first jets for commercial airlines. Soon, a flight from New York to London took only 7 hours

When my brother and I built and flew the first man-carrying flying machine, we thought that we were introducing into the world an invention which would make further wars practically impossible.
—Orville Wright

The Messerschmitt Me 262A-1 was the first jetfighter to see service in World War II.

The Boeing 747 is the largest passenger aircraft in the world. Weighing 315 tons, and able to carry more than 400 passengers, the 747 has changed the world of travel more than any other aircraft since the Wright brothers' 1903 Flyer.

instead of 14. In 1947, just two years after the war ended, American test pilot Chuck Yeager broke the sonic barrier by flying the rocket-powered Bell X-1 700 mph at 43,000 feet, which was faster than the speed of sound. In 1953, he flew a blazing 1,650 mph—more than twice the speed of sound!

These rocket-powered planes were followed by some of the first guided missiles and long-range rockets. Important advances in electronics combined with a greater knowledge of rocket engines and the physics of flight made these developments possible. The first Earth-orbiting satellites were quickly followed by larger and more complicated and useful satellites that circled the Earth every 90 minutes or hovered 23,000 miles above the planet in stationary orbit.

Engineers and designers created large rockets to fire nuclear warheads. Even larger rockets later carried the first astronauts and cosmonauts. Every person who piloted these rocket-powered craft and most of those who designed and built them had started with airplanes.

The next step was to combine a spacecraft and an airplane. The result was the space shuttle. This

The governments of France and the United Kingdom collaborated to construct the Concorde, the world's first supersonic commercial airliner. Traveling faster than the speed of sound, the Concorde can fly from New York to Paris in under four hours—less than half the time of the Boeing 747.

In the United States, the National Aeronautics and Space Administration (NASA) has developed the space shuttle for servicing satellites and conducting scientific research in outer space. The reusable shuttle returns to the Earth and lands like an airplane following a space mission. The rocket boosters that vertically propel the craft into space, however, fall into the ocean once their fuel has been exhausted, and they are not reusable.

craft takes off like a rocket, flies in space like a satellite, and then returns to Earth like an airplane.

One could say that, yes, humankind has indeed reached the sky: The sonic barrier has been broken, the moon has been reached, and the space shuttle has made space travel a fairly common occurrence. But the work is not done. The same inquisitive nature that inspired the Montgolfier brothers to fill bags with smoke and watch them rise will prompt humans to keep reaching beyond what is known.

NASA's latest project, the National AeroSpace Plane (NASP), might some day replace the space shuttle. It is hoped that the craft will be capable of transporting humans at Mach 25— more than 18,000 mph.

IMPORTANT EVENTS IN AVIATION HISTORY

1000 B.C.: Kites are flown in China.

ca. 400 B.C.: Archytas of Tarentum experiments with a model bird propelled by a jet of steam.

ca. 250 B.C.: Archimedes demonstrates the principle of buoyancy.

A.D. 1020: Tower jumper Eilmer attempts to fly with makeshift wings.

1260: Roger Bacon suggests that the principle of buoyancy would apply to balloons filled with "ethereal air."

1400s: Wind-up helicopter toys are available on the streets of Paris.

1480-1500: Leonardo da Vinci draws designs for helicopters, ornithopters, and parachutes.

1709: In Portugal, Bartolomeu Laurenco de Gusmão demonstrates a model hot-air balloon.

1765: James Watt develops a practical steam engine (patented in 1769).

1766: In England, hydrogen is discovered by Henry Cavendish.

1782: Joseph and Étienne Montgolfier begin their hot-air balloon experiments.

June 5, 1783: The Montgolfiers first demonstrate their balloon in public.

August 27, 1783: Jacques Alexandre César Charles publicly demonstrates the first hydrogen balloon.

September 19, 1783: In a Montgolfier balloon, a sheep, a rooster, and a duck become the first air passengers.

October 15, 1783: François Pilâtre de Rozier achieves the first human flight in a tethered hot-air balloon.

November 21, 1783: Rozier and the marquis d'Arlandes make the first free flight in a hot-air balloon.

December 1, 1783: J. A. C. Charles and Marie-Nöel Robert accomplish the first free flight in a hydrogen balloon.

January 7, 1785: John Jeffries and Jean Pierre Blanchard become the first to cross the English Channel in a balloon.

June 15, 1785: Rozier becomes the first aeronaut to die when his combination hydrogen and hot-air balloon explodes in midair.

1785: Jean-Baptiste Marie Meusnier designs his dirigible.

June 26, 1794: The French make the first use of an aircraft for military purposes with an observation balloon at the Battle of Fleurus.

October 22, 1797: The first parachute descent is made by a human.

1804: George Cayley flies his small glider.

1809-1810: Cayley publishes the first articles about heavier-than-air flight.

1842: W. H. Phillips flies his steam-powered model helicopter.

1842: William Henson designs his *Aerial Steam Carriage*.

1847: Henson and John Stringfellow fail in an attempt to fly a scale model of Henson's *Steam Carriage*.

1848: Stringfellow flies his steam-powered model airplane, reportedly as far as 120 feet.

1850: Pierre Jullien's clockwork-powered model dirigible flies.

128

September 24, 1852: Henri Giffard makes the first powered and controlled flight in a dirigible.

ca. 1853: Cayley's glider flies briefly with his coachman on board.

1853: François Letur builds and flies his parachute-type glider; he dies while attempting a flight the following year.

1855: Giffard crashes his second and last dirigible.

1857: Jean-Marie Le Bris builds and flies his albatross-like glider.

1861-1865: Directed by Thaddeus Lowe, balloons are used for observation by the North in the U.S. Civil War.

1867: Giffard creates a sensation at the Paris Exhibition by giving balloon rides to the public; during the same exhibition in 1878, he takes 35,000 people aloft.

1868: In London, at the first Aeronautical Exhibition, Stringfellow wins a prize for his steam engine.

1871: Alphonse Pénaud's rubber-band-powered model airplane flies.

1872: Dupuy-de-Lôme builds and flies his human-powered dirigible.

1874: Felix du Temple's steam-driven airplane performs a brief hop with a man on board, but it does not fly.

1883: Gaston and Albert Tissandier fly their electric-powered dirigible.

1884: Charles Renard and A. C. Krebs fly their electric-powered dirigible *La France*.

1884: Alexander Mozhaiski's large monoplane makes a brief hop down an incline, but it does not fly.

1885: Gottlieb Daimler perfects the gasoline-powered internal-combustion engine.

August 12, 1888: The first flight of a gasoline-powered aircraft is made by Karl Wölfert in his dirigible.

1889: Otto Lilienthal publishes *Birdflight as the Basis of Aviation*.

October 9, 1890: Clement Ader's bat-like *Eole* fails to fly when tested, but it does skim along the ground.

1891: Samuel Langley publishes *Experiments in Aerodynamics*.

1891: Lilienthal begins building and flying workable gliders.

July 31, 1894: Hiram Maxim attempts to fly his giant biplane, which rises from its guide track but does not fly.

1894: Lilienthal is the first human to be photographed in flight.

May 6, 1896: Langley's steam-powered *Aerodrome #5* achieves the first truly successful flight of a powered model airplane; six months later his *#6* flies 4,200 feet.

August 10, 1896: Lilienthal dies as the result of a gliding accident.

October 1897: Ader's *Avion III* fails to fly in repeated tests.

1898: Spanish-American War prompts the U.S. government to enlist Langley to develop an airplane for the military.

1898: Alberto Santos-Dumont begins his dirigible experiments with his airship *Number 1*.

1900: Orville and Wilbur Wright begin several years of gliding experiments near Kitty Hawk, North Carolina.

July 2, 1900: Count Zeppelin's first dirigible, *LZ-1*, flies briefly over Lake Constance.

October 19, 1901: Santos-Dumont circles the Eiffel Tower in his *Number 6* dirigible at 15 mph.

August 8, 1903: Langley's quarter-scale model *Aerodrome* makes the first flight of a gasoline-powered airplane.

October 7, 1903: With Charles Manly piloting, Langley's full-size *Aerodrome* crashes upon takeoff.

December 8, 1903: Manly crashes Langley's *Aerodrome* before achieving flight in his second and final attempt.

December 17, 1903: Orville Wright makes the first powered, sustained, and controlled heavier-than-air flight.

September 20, 1904: Wilbur Wright performs the first flight in a circle at Huffman Prairie near Dayton, Ohio.

November 12, 1906: Santos-Dumont makes the first powered and sustained airplane flight in Europe.

September 29, 1907: Louis Breguet's helicopter becomes the first to lift off the ground in a tethered flight with a human on board.

October 1, 1907: Alexander Graham Bell organizes the Aerial Experiment Association (AEA).

November 13, 1907: Paul Cornu achieves the first free flight of a helicopter with a human on board.

March 12, 1908: The AEA's first aircraft, *Drome Number 1* (*Red Wing*), crashes after flying more than 318 feet.

May 22, 1908: In his first attempt at airplane flight, Glenn Curtiss flies the AEA's *White Wing* more than 1,000 feet.

July 4, 1908: Curtiss flies the AEA's *June Bug* farther than the required distance of one kilometer to win the *Scientific American* Trophy.

September 17, 1908: Orville Wright crashes while making a demonstration flight for the U.S. Army. His passenger, Thomas Selfridge, is killed in the crash.

November 1908: Curtiss fits the AEA's *June Bug* with pontoons, but the craft fails to take off from the water.

1909: Igor Sikorsky travels to France and is exposed to the budding field of aviation; he builds his first helicopter.

July 17, 1909: Curtiss wins his second *Scientific American* Trophy for flying in a circle for 25 miles.

July 25, 1909: Louis Blériot becomes the first to cross the English Channel in an airplane.

August 2, 1909: The U.S. Army buys its first airplane—a Wright biplane.

August 29, 1909: Curtiss wins the Gordon Bennett Cup at the first international air meet in Rheims, France.

February 1910: Sikorsky builds his second unsuccessful helicopter.

March 28, 1910: In his seaplane, Henri Fabre becomes the first to take off from and land on water.

May 29, 1910: Curtiss flies 150 miles along the Hudson River from Albany to New York City to win the *New York World* prize.

November 14, 1910: Eugene Ely takes off in a Curtiss plane from the deck of the USS *Birmingham.*

February 17, 1911: Curtiss lands his seaplane alongside the USS *Pennsylvania* and is hauled aboard.

May 17, 1911: Sikorsky flies his first successful airplane, the *S-5;* the *S-6* follows in 1912.

July 1, 1911: The first flight of a U.S. Navy aircraft, a Curtiss seaplane

November 5, 1911: Flying a Wright biplane, Calbraith Rodgers completes the first North American coast-to-coast flight.

May 13, 1913: Sikorsky's *Grand,* the first four-engined airplane, flies; his four-engined *Ilia Mourometz* series follows.

May 28, 1914: Glenn Curtiss flies Langley's rebuilt *Aerodrome* over Lake Keuka in New York.

June 28, 1914: Archduke Francis Ferdinand of Austria-Hungary is assassinated, igniting World War I.

January 15, 1915: The first air raid on Britain by Germany's Zeppelin airships

1917: In the Russian Revolution, the Bolsheviks come to power under Lenin.

March 30, 1919: Sikorsky arrives in the United States after fleeing Russia.

May 27, 1919: With stops to refuel, the *NC-4* flying boat becomes the first aircraft to cross the Atlantic Ocean.

June 14-15, 1919: First direct nonstop flight across the Atlantic achieved by British pilots J. Alcock and A. Brown.

January 9, 1923: Juan de la Cierva's autogiro becomes the first rotary-winged craft to fly under the complete control of the pilot.

March 5, 1923: Sikorsky organizes the Sikorsky Aero Engineering Corporation in New York City.

September 4, 1923: The first helium-filled airship, the *Shenandoah,* flies in the United States.

May 21, 1927: Charles Lindbergh completes the first nonstop solo flight across the Atlantic Ocean.

August 8-29, 1929: The *Graf Zeppelin* achieves the first around-the-world flight by an airship.

1930: Frank Whittle is granted a patent for his jet-engine design.

May 20, 1932: Amelia Earhart is the first woman to fly solo across the Atlantic.

July 15-22, 1933: Wiley Post achieves the first solo around-the-world flight.

January 12, 1935: Amelia Earhart is the first person to fly solo across the Pacific Ocean, from Hawaii to California.

1935: Although it lacked suitable control, Breguet's helicopter flies to 500 feet.

June 26, 1936: The first flight of the Fa-61, the world's first practical helicopter

1937: The Fa-61 flies for a world record of more than 1 hour and 20 minutes; Hanna Reitsch makes several indoor exhibition flights with the craft the following year.

May 6, 1937: The German zeppelin *Hindenburg* crashes at Lakehurst, New Jersey, effectively ending lighter-than-air passenger travel.

June 20, 1938: German test pilot Karl Bode flies the Fa-61 a record 143 miles.

June 20, 1939: The Heinkel He 176 is the first rocket-powered airplane to fly.

August 27, 1939: The first flight of a jet-powered airplane is achieved by the Heinkel He 178.

September 1939: World War II begins.

March 13, 1940: Sikorsky makes the first free flight in his VS-300.

May 6, 1941: Sikorsky stays aloft in the VS-300 for 1 hour, 32 minutes, and 26.1 seconds to establish a new world record.

December 7, 1941: Japanese air attack on the U.S. naval base at Pearl Harbor prompts the U.S. to enter World War II.

January 1942: Sikorsky XR-4, or R-4, first flies; the R-5 and R-6 follow.

1945: World War II ends.

October 14, 1947: U.S. Air Force test pilot Chuck Yeager flies the Bell X-1 to Mach 1.07, becoming the first human to fly faster than the speed of sound.

June 26, 1948: The Berlin airlift begins.

1950-1953: Korean War; first war in which helicopters play a major role

May 2, 1952: The De Havilland Comet becomes first jet-powered aircraft to offer regular passenger service.

May 18, 1953: Jacqueline Cochran is the first woman to break the sound barrier.

December 12, 1953: Yeager flies the Bell X-1A at Mach 2.5, more than twice the speed of sound.

October 4, 1957: Russian spacecraft *Sputnik I* becomes the first satellite to be launched into the Earth's orbit.

October 22, 1960: American Ed Yost first flies his nylon hot-air balloon developed for the U.S. Navy.

April 12, 1961: Russian cosmonaut Yuri Gagarin becomes the first human to travel in space in the spaceship *Vostok I*.

1962: Sikorsky's heavy-lifting S-64 Skycrane goes into production.

February 9, 1969: The first flight of the Boeing 747, the first jet-powered wide-body airliner

March 2, 1969: The first flight of the prototype of the supersonic-transport (SST) aircraft Concorde

July 21, 1969: U.S. astronaut Neil Armstrong becomes the first human to walk on the moon.

May 14, 1973: *Skylab,* an earth-orbiting space station that allowed people to live in space for several weeks, is launched.

January 21, 1976: The supersonic Concorde begins commercial service.

July 20, 1976: *Viking 1* spacecraft lands on Mars and sends back pictures to Earth.

April 12, 1981: The first flight of the U.S. space shuttle *Columbia*

February 20, 1986: Russian space station *Mir* is launched, allowing cosmonauts to stay in space for record lengths of time.

April 24, 1990: The Hubble space telescope is launched, opening space to new levels of scientific exploration.

January 1991: In Operation Desert Storm, the stealth combat airplane is first used.

July 1997: The unmanned Sojourner rover travels the surface of Mars and sends back data on soil and rock composition.

GLOSSARY

aerial: relating to flight or aircraft

aerodrome: a French word for airport or airfield; used by Samuel Langley and others as a synonym for "airplane"

aerodynamics: the science of air in motion and the motion of objects in air

aeronaut: one who flies in a lighter-than-air craft

aeronautics: the science or art of flight

aerostat: an unpowered, lighter-than-air craft, such as a hot-air balloon

aerostation: the science of lighter-than-air flight

ailerons: the movable flaps on the wings of an airplane that are used to control rolling and banking

airfoil: the cross-section shape of an airplane's wing or tail that produces lift

airship: a powered, steerable lighter-than-air craft (also called a dirigible) such as a blimp or zeppelin; *see also* **balloon**

altimeter: an aircraft instrument used for determining altitude

altitude: the height of an object above a given level, such as feet above sea level

amphibian: an aircraft that can take off from and land on either land or water

arresting gear: a device used to bring aircraft to a stop when landing on an aircraft carrier or other seacraft

astronaut: a person trained to participate in the flight of a spacecraft

autogiro: an aircraft that is driven forward by a propeller and derives lift from an unpowered rotor mounted above the fuselage.

aviator: the pilot of a glider, airplane, or helicopter

ballast: a weight, generally sand or water, carried in a lighter-than-air aircraft to allow variation in lift; throwing off, or jettisoning, ballast makes a craft lighter and increases lift

balloon: an unpowered and unsteerable lighter-than-air craft; *see also* **airship**

bank: the lateral tilting or leaning of an aircraft, usually while turning

biplane: an airplane with two sets of main wings, one above the other; *see also* **monoplane** and **triplane**

blimp: a generally non-rigid airship

cabin: an enclosed compartment for the passengers of an aircraft

camber: the curvature of an airfoil surface; cambered wings produce lift

carbonic-acid gas: a weak, unstable substance found in solutions of carbon dioxide in water; used by Otto Lilienthal to fuel his ornithopter engine

catapult: a mechanism used to launch aircraft at a speed sufficient for flight, as from the deck of an aircraft carrier

coal gas: a lighter-than-air gaseous mixture released by burning coal

cockpit: the compartment, generally at the front of the cabin, from which the pilot and crew control an aircraft

coke: a material derived from processed coal that can be burned as fuel

control: the ability to direct an aircraft in turning, banking, diving, and climbing

control surface: a surface that provides control for an airplane, such as the rudder, ailerons, and elevator

cosmonaut: the Russian equivalent of the English "astronaut"

dirigible: another term for airship; from the Latin *dirigere*, to direct

drag: the resistance of air against the moving structure of an aircraft

elevator: the movable control surface used to direct the ascent and descent of an aircraft; *see also* **rudder**

envelope: the container that holds either gas or hot air in a lighter-than-air aircraft; *see also* **gasbag**

fixed-wing craft: an aircraft with lift provided by wings that are rigid, or fixed, and do not move

float plane: a seaplane that operates from water and is supported by pontoons

flying boat: a seaplane with a hull-shaped fuselage that acts as a flotation surface

free flight: a flight in which the craft is not restricted by ropes; *see also* **tethered flight**

fuselage: the body of an aircraft

gasbag: a bag that contains the lifting gas in a lighter-than-air craft

glider: an unpowered, heavier-than-air, fixed-wing aircraft used for gliding or soaring; *see also* **sailplane**

gondola: a basket or enclosure suspended beneath a balloon or dirigible to hold passengers or cargo

hang glider: a glider in which the pilot hangs below the wings and controls direction by moving the legs and body

heavier-than-air flight: flight of a craft, such as an airplane, that weighs more than air; lift is derived from wings; *see also* **lighter-than-air flight**

helicopter: an aircraft that derives lift and thrust from powered rotor blades; it can hover and take off and land without a runway

helium: a light, nonflammable gaseous element, used to provide lift for balloons and airships

hover: to float or remain suspended in air

hull: the fuselage of a flying boat

hydrogen: a colorless, highly flammable gas; the lightest of all lifting gases used for lighter-than-air flight

internal-combustion engine: an engine that burns fuel within a confined space and converts the released energy into mechanical power; *see also* **piston engine**

jet engine: an engine in which air and fuel are burned together in a combustion chamber; the resulting jet of exhaust produces thrust and drives an aircraft forward

landplane: a heavier-than-air craft that operates only from land

lift: the upward force that results from an airstream passing over an airfoil such as a wing

lighter-than-air flight: flight of a craft in which lift is provided by substances such as gases or hot air that are lighter than regular air; *see also* **heavier-than-air flight**

Mach: the ratio of an aircraft's speed to the speed of sound; Mach 1 is the speed of sound, or 760 mph at sea level (it decreases with greater altitude), Mach 2 is twice the speed of sound, and so forth; named for Austrian physicist Ernst Mach

monoplane: an airplane with only one set of wings; *see also* **biplane** and **triplane**

ornithopter: an aircraft that is held aloft and propelled by flapping wings

parachute: an umbrella-like device used to slow descent from an aircraft by providing resistance to air

payload: the total weight of passengers and cargo that an aircraft can carry

piston engine: an internal-combustion engine in which small explosions push pistons back and forth within a cylinder to produce mechanical power; radial, in-line, and V-type engines are types of piston engines

propeller: rotating blades, driven by an engine, that propel an aircraft forward; once called airscrews

prototype: the first working example of a new machine, often built for testing before producing the machines in large quantities

rotary engine: an early piston engine with cylinders that spin around a fixed crankshaft to drive a propeller

rotor: an assembly of rotating horizontal airfoils, or blades, that provides lift for helicopters and autogiros

rudder: a movable control surface that directs horizontal (left and right) movement; *see also* **elevator**

runway: a strip of level, usually paved, ground from which aircraft can take off and land

sailplane: a high-performance glider

scale model: a model based on the design for a full-size machine but with dimensions that are reduced proportionately

seaplane: a heavier-than-air craft that operates only from water; *see also* **float plane** and **flying boat**

stall: the condition of an aircraft that loses lift and is unable to maintain altitude

static: having no motion; stationary

supersonic: travel at speeds exceeding the speed of sound

tail-rotor: a rotor mounted on the tail of a helicopter to counteract torque; also called an anti-torque rotor

tandem-winged: a fixed-wing craft with wings that are arranged one behind the other

test-bed: a mechanism built to test or measure the forces and effectiveness of airfoils, rotors, or engines

tethered flight: a restricted flight in which the aircraft is tied to the ground; *see also* **free flight**

thrust: the force, or **power**, developed by a propeller or jet engine to drive an aircraft forward

torque: a turning or twisting force caused by the spinning of an aircraft's propeller or rotor

triplane: an airplane with wings placed one above the other on three levels; *see also* **biplane** and **monoplane**

turbine: any of various machines in which the energy of a moving fluid, such as gas or water, is converted to mechanical power

turbojet: a jet engine with a turbine-driven compressor that develops thrust from the exhaust of hot gases

variable-pitch propeller: a propeller in which the pitch, or angle, of the blades can be changed to optimize performance

VTOL: Vertical TakeOff and Landing; a craft that is capable of taking off and landing by moving straight up or down

wingspan: the distance between the wingtips of an aircraft or bird

wing warping: a method of twisting wings to control rolling and banking; used by the Wright brothers; replaced by ailerons in modern aircraft

zeppelin: a rigid airship held aloft by internal gas cells; named for its inventor, Count Ferdinand von Zeppelin

BIBLIOGRAPHY

Above and Beyond: The Encyclopedia of Aviation and Space Sciences. Chicago: New Horizons, 1967.

Angelucci, Enzo. *The Rand McNally Encyclopedia of Civil Aircraft.* Chicago: Rand McNally, 1982.

————. *The Rand McNally Encyclopedia of Military Aircraft.* Chicago: Rand McNally, 1983.

Berliner, Don. *Before the Wright Brothers.* Minneapolis: Lerner, 1990.

Bilstein, Roger E. *Flight in America, 1900-1983: From the Wrights to the Astronauts.* Baltimore: The Johns Hopkins University Press, 1984.

Bonney, Walter T. *The Heritage of Kitty Hawk.* New York: Norton,1962.

Bryan, C. D. B. *The National Air and Space Museum.* 2nd ed. New York: Abrams, 1988.

Carey, Keith. *The Helicopter: An Illustrated History.* Wellingborough, England: Patrick Stevens, 1986.

Cochrane, Dorothy, Von Hardesty, and Russell Lee. *The Aviation Careers of Igor Sikorsky.* Seattle: University of Washington Press, 1989.

Crouch, Tom D. *The Eagle Aloft: Two Centuries of the Balloon in America.* Washington, D.C.: Smithsonian Institution Press, 1983.

Delear, Frank J. *Igor Sikorsky: His Three Careers in Aviation.* New York: Dodd, Mead, 1976.

"The Flying Man." *McClure's,* September 1894, 323-31.

Freedman, Russell. *The Wright Brothers: How They Invented the Airplane.* New York: Holiday House, 1991.

Gibbs-Smith, Charles H. *A History of Flying.* New York: Frederick A. Praeger, 1954.

Gillespie, Charles C. *Dictionary of Scientific Biography.* New York: Scribner's, 1974.

Gordon, Arthur. *The American Heritage History of Flight*. New York: Aviation Heritage, 1962.

Gunston, Bill, ed. *Chronicle of Aviation*. London: Chronicle Communications, 1992.

Hatch, Alden. *Glenn Curtiss: Pioneer of Naval Aviation*. New York: Messner, 1942.

Howard, Fred. *Wilbur and Orville: A Biography of the Wright Brothers*. New York: Knopf, 1987.

Lilienthal, Otto. "Why Is Artificial Flight So Difficult of Invention?" *American Engineer and Railroad Journal*, December 1894, 575-78.

Mondey, David I., ed. *The International Encyclopedia of Aviation*. New York: Crown, 1977.

Moser, Barry. *Fly! A Brief History of Flight Illustrated*. New York: HarperCollins, Willa Perlman Books, 1993.

Munson, Kenneth. *Flying Boats and Seaplanes since 1909*. New York: Macmillan, 1971.

Scharf, Robert, and Walter S. Taylor. *Over Land and Sea: A Biography of Glenn Hammond Curtiss*. New York: McKay, 1968.

Stockbridge, Frank P. "Glenn Curtiss" (a four-part series). *Popular Science Monthly*, March 1927, April 1927, May 1927, June 1927.

Taylor, John. "The Man Who Didn't Invent the Airplane." *Yankee*, November 1981, 144-47; 222-29.

Taylor, Michael J. H., David Mondey, and John W. R. Taylor. *The Guinness Book of Air Facts and Feats*. London: Guinness Superlatives, 1973.

Wescott, Lyanne, and Paula Degen. *Wind and Sand: The Story of the Wright Brothers at Kitty Hawk*. New York: Abrams, 1983.

Wolko, Howard S. *In the Cause of Flight: Technologists of Aeronautics and Astronautics*. Washington, D.C.: Smithsonian Institution Press, 1981.

INDEX

Académie des Sciences (National Academy of the Sciences), 16
Ader, Clement, 59, 61
Aerial Experiment Association (AEA), 91, 92, 93, 96
Aerial Steam Carriage, 55-57
Aero Club of America, 92, 96
aerodrome, 67, 91, 92, 93
Aerodrome, 63-67, 68, 69, 83
Aerodrome #5, 63, 64
Aeronautical Exhibition, 57
ailerons, 10, 92, 93
Air Force Museum, U.S., 119
airplanes, 9, 11, 28, 36, 39, 41, 76, 97, 98; built by AEA, 91-93; built by Langley, 63-67, 68; built by Sikorsky, 109-112; built by Wright brothers, 79-85, 86-87; early development of, 44, 54, 55, 57-62, 72; jet, 122-24; model, 55, 56, 58, 63, 64, 67, 68, 72; scientific method of designing, 50, 71-72, 75; used during World War II, 103, 121-122, 123. *See also* seaplane
air pressure, 41
airscrew, 105
airship, 25, 27-28, 32, 33, 34, 36, 37, 39, 66, 90; power for, 27-29, 30-31, 34, 36, 38-39. *See also* dirigible, zeppelin
albatross, 42
Allies, 112, 123
Amécourt, viscomte de Ponton d', 106
America, 102, 103
amphibian, 97, 112
Anzani engine, 108, 113
Archimedes, 15
Archytas of Tarentum, 8
Army, U.S., 91, 98, 112, 113, 116, 117, 119
Army Air Corps, U.S., 116
astronauts, 125
astronomy, 62
autogiro, 115
automobile, 36, 74, 80, 91

Avion III, 61

Bacon, Roger, 9
Baldwin, Frederick "Casey," 92
Baldwin, Thomas, 90-91, 92
ballast, 22, 24
balloon, hot-air, 9, 11, 24, 25, 27, 45, 54, 75, 97; animals carried by, 19-20; early experiments with, 14-15, 16; humans carried by, 21; lift of, provided by heated air, 15, 16, 17; used for recreation, 25
balloon, hydrogen, 17, 18, 22, 23, 24, 25, 33, 36, 54
balloon, tethered, 20, 24-25, 33
Balzer, Stephen, 64, 65
banking, 64, 76, 79, 92
barnstormers, 122
bat, 61
batteries, 34, 35, 106
Bell, Alexander Graham, 64, 91, 92
Bell X-1, 124
bicycle, 73, 89, 90
biplane, 59-60, 121-122; glider, 46, 75, 76; kite, 75, 76
Birdflight as the Basis of Aviation, 45
birds, 27, 28, 44, 50; as models for human flight, 8-9, 10, 45, 46, 47-48, 54, 71, 75, 105; wings of, 41, 42, 43, 45, 50
Birmingham USS, 99
Blanchard, Jean Pierre, 24
Blériot, Louis, 96, 108
blimp, 39
Bode, Karl, 114
Boeing: Clipper, 121; *747*, 124, 125
bolometer, 62
Bolsheviks, 111, 112
Bothezat, George de, 113
Breguet, Louis, 107, 113
Breguet-Dorand 314, 113
British European Airways, 118
buoyancy, 15

ABOUT THE AUTHOR

Don Berliner is the author of nearly two dozen books and hundreds of magazine articles about aviation and space exploration. As a race official, photographer, and reporter, he has attended numerous air racing and aerobatic events throughout the United States as well as in England, Scotland, France, Hungary, Czechoslovakia (now the Czech Republic), and the Ukraine. Berliner lives in Alexandria, Virginia, where he is the editor of *Golden Pylons*, the newsletter of the Society of Air Racing Historians. He is a member of the Experimental Aircraft Association and the International Association of Aviation Historians.

PHOTO ACKNOWLEDGEMENTS

The Boeing Company Archives: p. 124
Catchpenny Prints: p. 9
Don Berliner: p. 125
Dover Dictionary of American Portraits: p. 51
Famous Nineteenth-Century Faces: p. 64
Frank Leslie's Popular Monthly Magazine: pp. 10, 43
Glenn H. Curtiss Museum: pp. 69, 88, 92, 94, 95, 100, 122
Library of Congress: pp. 6, 7, 12, 17, 19, 20, 23, 24, 30, 37, 44, 46, 48, 50, 57, 61, 70, 73 (both), 74, 76, 78, 81, 86, 87, 96, 106, 111, 112, 120
Meyer's Lexicon: p. 65
Minnesota Historical Society: p. 18

National Aeronautics and Space Administration: p. 126
National Air and Space Museum, Smithsonian Institution: pp. 14 (both), 21, 26, 36, 38, 40, 52, 54 (both), 56, 58, 67, 98, 107, 110, 114, 117
Ready-to-Use Old-Fashioned Transportation Cuts: pp. 11, 31, 34
Sikorsky Aircraft Corporation: pp. 104, 116
Transportation: A Pictorial Archive from Nineteenth-Century Sources: pp. 8, 25, 28, 29, 35, 60
U.S. Air Force: pp. 123, 127
U.S. Navy (Courtesy of National Museum of Naval Aviation)**:** pp. 99, 101, 102, 119

J629.13 Berliner, Don

   Avation: Reaching for the s
   sky.

10/99   c. 1997

Georgetown Peabody Library
Lincoln Park
Georgetown, Massachusetts 01833
Please do not remove date due card